# The Pattern *of* Your Life

*A Memoir of Growing Up in the 50's*

# JUDY ARMSTRONG

I am firmly convinced that you can't see the pattern of your life until you've reached a ripe old age of say 75 or so. It takes three quarters of a century to give you perspective. All the things that occurred—all the dilemmas you found yourself in, all the tragedies, joys, failures and triumphs—actually form a woven tapestry and happened to you for a reason. I like to think that many, many times an event which seemed tragic at the time was actually going to be the seed bed for something wonderful which could have never taken place without it!

Herein I attempt to share my insights with the reader and ask, after finishing these chapters, if he agrees!

# I.

# Early Life

# My Parents

Both of my parents went to the University of Illinois, which was odd in that Dad was from Nebraska and Mother from Indiana. The time period was the early 30's and our country was about to get deep into a historic depression. Dad explained that his father thought that an engineering degree was the path to future success. (see Presidents Hoover's biography) and mammoth bridges and skyscrapers were awesome!

Dad almost died because he was the epitome (or nadir) of the square peg in a round hole. He told me that you had to draw a corrugated box lid and, using math, figure out just how to draw it if it were crumpled in a certain way. He almost never went to class, so when it was test time he literally burned the midnight oil and was able to get a passing grade! So, he was sent by his parents to Illinois because of its engineering classes.

Mother told me that it was a nice distance from Indiana and she looked forward to meeting new friends and not just going off to an Indiana college and having it feel like an extension of high school with many of the same people.

Magic happened the night that the Kappa's invited the Phi Psi's over to their sorority house for a party!

Dad said he was talking to his date in the hall at the bottom of the staircase when he looked up and saw a vision of white (Mother) on the landing. He didn't want to be rude so he desperately thought of what he could say to get rid of his date and go meet Mother.

Apparently, they hit it off and he called for "Coke dates" so they could meet between classes. Mother figured out a way to meet during her physical education class. She had an aversion to anything at all physical anyway and she said when she walked in this enormous gymnasium and saw all these thick ropes dangling from a distant ceiling and these sawhorse things that it filled her with dread, so she had a sorority sister answer "Here!" when her name was called.

Everything went very smoothly until one day she was instructed to meet with the teacher who said, "I can't understand this, Jane. You've been here every day, but you haven't accomplished anything!"

Mother also told me that she was looking for a "crip" (easy) course, to take to fill a schedule slot so Dad, anxious to be helpful, advised her to take a poetry class. (He actually wrote poetry from time to time.) Well, she was never so flummoxed! She said, "The poem was talking about lilacs blooming in a dooryard, but it was actually about the death of President Lincoln." She couldn't understand the symbolism as she was very literal and (as she often said), uncreative and unimaginative. It made absolutely no sense to her and Dad had to help her with every poem in the course!

When she pledged Kappa Kappa Gamma she was really terrified because all the pledges had to write and perform skits and she just knew she couldn't create one, but the sisters were quick to reassure her by chiming in, "Just sing, Jane!" Mother was so relieved! She came from a very musical family and could she sing! As I always said, "She could really sell a song!" Her timing and her beautiful alto voice were superb. She especially loved Cole Porter and George Gershwin but she knocked 'em dead with "It Had to Be You" and "There'll Be Some Changes Made."

The following year she saw what went on with the sisters when they voted on the next crop of pledges. She said as the night wore on and the girls were tiring, they would take on a chant, "Not Kappa material" with every name that came up. This horrified her as being so very unfair.

Mother was a lifelong Kappa, though, and had a beautiful key pin encrusted with pearls that I have now. She attended every luncheon and meeting that she possibly could and had many Kappa friends.

As the terrible Depression deepened, both of my parents left college without graduating, and my father, who had won an art scholarship in high school, decided to go conquer New York by going to Art Students' League there.

He said he quickly found out that when he went from the little pond in Omaha to the big pond in New York, he was one of many, many talented artists—just one—and he was not going to conquer the world.

Not too long after that, my parents got married in Indianapolis. My mother's family lived there. They chose Uncle Mike and Aunt Kate's classic home and had a fairly small wedding of very good friends and family. There was a harpist on the stair landing! Mother chose a beautiful blue dress instead of the customary white since it was the depression and she could get many more wearings out of it.

They were so fortunate to be able to go on a honeymoon in those dreadful times! Mother carefully saved the bill from the hotel in Chicago that was, I believe, $12.95. Then off they motored to my father's family's summer cabin on a lake in the wilds of Minnesota. There was Mother, who had never cooked, much less scaled a fish or cut off its head, dealing with her new life. (I never heard much about the honeymoon.)

When it was over, off they went to Omaha, where Dad had a job as a commercial artist. Mother missed her family and friends, I'm sure, and one of the things she missed most was big shade trees. Nebraska was a plains state, and if you wanted trees, you planted them. There were miles and miles of corn and wheat as far as the eye could see, but nary a tree You can cross bridges in Omaha and look down at bodies of black Angus and red Herefords squirming below and bellowing, too. It just wasn't her scene. She seemed lonely and my Dad decided that what she needed was a baby!

They lived in the Kipling Apartments and, of course, air conditioning hadn't been invented and Omaha had the hottest summer on record in 1936. Mother liked even numbers for birthdays and was happy that when I arrived it was September 18! There she lay in that hot hospital trying to nurse me but the nurses told her that her milk wasn't rich enough so the solution was to drink beer. Mother loved beer so Dad started hauling it in!

When I was about three we moved in with Nana Gallup, my father's mother, who had recently divorced her husband and was having a lot of difficulties being on her own. My outstanding memories included getting royally lost and only the fact that my parents had drilled Nana's address into my head saved me. With each corner I turned my panic increased. Nothing looked familiar. A police car drove up and a cop put me in and asked where I lived. I replied without hesitation, "Eleven-o-nine South 36th St." (I think that was it). They pulled up in front and asked, "Is this your house?" as we were all walking up the front walk. I answered "no" because it was my grandmother's house. They whirled me around and started to beat a hasty retreat when my parents appeared on the front porch waving their arms and shouting at me.

Dad's younger brother, Uncle Paul, delighted in making up off-color lines for nursery rhymes and drilling his versions into my head which I would then recite at formal dinner parties in the dining room while he giggled away.

Dad's sister, Aunt Ginny, was a talented artist like my father and she actually wrote a little book of her own creation for me, illustrated it with cute cartoons of animals and gave it to me as a surprise. She was very popular and surrounded by high school friends who were always driving over. They would pop me into their convertibles and off we would all go!

Aunt Ginny once went to a picnic with Andy Rooney, but that time I didn't go. Darn! I could have told you that I met a movie star before I was even in kindergarten.

Mrs. Hoy lived next door. She liked me and I used to visit her. She was very hard of hearing and didn't catch everything I said. I was telling her about my first airplane ride and all of my impressions and wound up by saying that I had gone to the bathroom, too. She asked, apparently not hearing this, "Did it make any noise?" I responded, "I didn't, but the airplane did!"

I learned the meaning of the term "approach-avoidance" one Sunday when I had charged off on my tricycle to play with a friend without checking first with Mother or Dad. They called everyone they could think of trying to find me and when they did my Father said very sternly on the phone, "You come right home as fast as your little legs can carry you!"

As I grew, I was quite "willful" as Mother wrote in my baby book. (Think "hard headed, bossy brat"). My one saving grace, apparently, was caring for young children. Apparently, I was quite protective of them; nevertheless, I was dubbed "L'Enfant Terrible" behind my back.

We had moved to a duplex on one of the busiest

streets – Leavenworth – and acquired a little black cocker spaniel puppy. One day a truck ran over him in the alley behind our home and I can clearly remember Mother sobbing and my comforting her—at age 3!

A bully lived next day—Buddy by name—and he threatened me all the time if I didn't do everything he said, so one day Mother gasped when she looked out and saw me riding my trike in circles in the very busy Leavenworth street – over the street car tracks. I got a real spanking, but I didn't think it was fair since Buddy made me do that!

My favorite playmate lived across another busy street, so I was forbidden to ever cross it. Of course, I did, and we had fun riding our tricycles together. When my parents found out, they tried spankings and then once sent me to bed without any dinner. That stressed Mother out severely and she kept sneaking up and checking on me. Finally, after another of my secret visits to Billy's house, they decided to tie me to the clothes pole. This was one of those sturdy T-shaped metal varieties in the back yard. When Mother looked out I had untied the ropes, climbed to the top, and was walking across the top of the pole.

I was probably around four when we moved into a wonderful white brick cape cod on an acre or two in the outskirts of Omaha. It was a lovely rural kind of neighborhood, then, called "Loveland." It had crushed rock roads and rolling terrain and its own little school house about three blocks away.

This was paradise for a young child! Behind us were tall cornfields. I can still hear their dry, rustling sound as the wind whipped through them. Next to us were huge sunflowers, over my head like the cornstalks, and way back behind all the waving corn was pioneer land to discover! There was a burned-out skeleton of a cabin with a chimney, charred but whole, sporting one nail on which a rusty tin cup hung. My sense of history and thrill of being perhaps the first person to see that since pioneer days in Nebraska stirred deep within me.

I ventured further and found a cliff and a muddy creek. It seemed to my young mind that the world had no boundaries but went on and on! This was a precious discovery for my spirit and as an adult I look back on those years as being very formative, very positive, and I wish all children could have such an exhilarating sense of freedom.

Life was idyllic in every way. We went out to Boy's Town where my Dad introduced me to Father Flanagan, a wonderful man who headed it up. He personally gave us two dalmatians who were brother and sister. We named them "Pat and Mike" because it was an Irish sort of pairing, I guess. Later, my grandfather would always say, "Pat and Mike, they look alike." They played happily together in the setting we provided and gave me so much pleasure.

# World War II

Born in 1936, I was a WWII baby, and as such, I learned many valuable life lessons!

We lived on an acre in an outlying neighborhood in Omaha called "Loveland" and the neighbors were wonderful people who all pulled together during the war and freely lent their resources to others. They often had cook-outs in each other's back yards on those permanent brick ovens with chimneys—I can just see them—with the host providing all the side dishes and the neighbors bringing their own meat. This was made easy since all had big vegetable gardens and strawberry bushes. Gas was rationed, of course, as were sugar, rubber and shoes that I remember. People tore stamps out of little ration books. I'm sure times were rough, but you never knew it from watching all the fun our friends and neighbors had. They played bridge and walked to each other's homes to do so and they sang around our piano for hours! Many of the songs my dad played were college tunes from everyone's alma mater followed by those patriotic songs: "Off We Go Into the Wild Blue Yonder," "And Russia Is Her Name,"

"Anchors Away," "From the Halls of Monte Zuma" and "Mary's a Grand Old Name," for one of our neighbors, and always "I'd Love to Live in Loveland" which was the name of our neighborhood. Great free fun!

I did homework in the living room next to the radio, so I could hear my stories when they came on at 5: "Hop Harrigan, Ace of The Airways," "Captain Midnight," "Jack Armstrong, The All-American Boy" to name a few. They held me spellbound!

We played patriotic games about being Junior Commandos and made paper armbands with those words written on them. Outside we would tie the tops of sunflowers together and call them our forts.

We got lost in fields of corn over our heads behind the houses. It was a short distance to my friend Cynthia's house if I cut through those tall cornstalks, but sometimes I got confused and came out a mile from where she lived!

It's a wonderful thing to grow up with no concrete, no sidewalks to hem you in.

I had a wagon to pull around the neighborhood to look for treasures that could be used in the war effort. Tin foil from gum wrappers were rolled into balls, scrap metal of any kind was rescued. Pickings were lean, but we tried!

At school the recesses were spent playing war games. I wanted to fight with a gun, but all the girls were supposed to be nurses! Boring!

Other recesses we gathered milkweed pods in the field next to our school to be used in flotation in life vests, and rafts! This was exciting to me—a real tangible contribution.

We bought war stamps and war bonds at school. I remember the long tables where they were sold.

My Dad really wanted to be in the Navy but one eye wasn't up to par. (He wore glasses). I remember his efforts to improve his vision, including drinking gallons of carrot juice and following a flashlight beam on the wall of a darkened basement. Interestingly, he actually did improve that eye but not enough to get in. (Mother was relieved).

Mother did everything a stay-at-home Mom could do. She sent me off to school with money for war bonds and stamps. She learned every rank in all the services and probably knew their battle ribbons, too. I know she knew what the medals stood for.

She went off to knitting classes and I remember boxes of scarves and gloves for "the poor dumb Russians" as she called them and of course the "Knittin' for Britain" campaign which she heartily endorsed, being a strong Anglophile.

# Father

Dad would come home from his work at Bozell and Jacobs, a multi-state advertising firm where he began as a commercial artist and eventually became a vice president and branch manager. But I'm ahead of myself.

He would come home and plunge into gardening, a life-long passion. It was World War II and America had, of course, entered in 1941 after the terrible "Day of Infamy," as Roosevelt so eloquently put it. This was the reason for his enormous victory garden. I really think he could have supplied the SAC base, plus our immediate neighborhood! This was my first experience with the wonderful taste of fresh picked vegetables. I especially loved the warm tomatoes right off the vine!

He also planted a beautiful flower garden and then decided that the curved bank behind the driveway just had to become a rock garden. That man spent hours and hours laboring in it!

Not only did our country go to war in 1941 but that year also marked my entrance into kindergarten, sharpening my reading skills, and – lo and behold! A sister was born on my birthday! I said, "I love all of my presents, but this is the best present of all!"

Nana Fansler, my mother's mother, came on the train from Indianapolis to help Mother with the new baby. There is a picture of me with her on our front porch holding a small, flat one-layer cake on that memorable day.

It was during this time period that a guardian angel was smiling down on our family. Nana never went to the doctor (nor did my Mother except during her pregnancy and follow-up). Nana told her that she was experiencing constant bleeding and Mother said, "You must come to the doctor with me tomorrow—that's not normal!" It was discovered, way back then, that she had uterine cancer that was successfully treated and she lived from her age then (44) to a ripe old 84. I am certain that she never would have taken action if she hadn't been there with Mother.

Shortly after my sister was born my friends would want to come over and see the new baby. I would retort, "Why? She just lies there!"

Unfortunately, no one had prepared me in any way for a new baby in the house, so at least I thought I would instantly have a built-in playmate.

But other things were wonderful in my life! Nana Fansler, my maternal grandmother, took me back to

Indianapolis to visit with her and "Bopa," my name for grandfather. I wanted to sleep on the upper berth in our bedroom on the train, but Nana was afraid I'd fall out. She finally gave in as she always did with me. We were real buddies.

They lived in a wonderful apartment high in the sky with buzzers you got to ring and speak to the person you wanted to visit, and a neat underground garage. I got to pick whatever cereal I wanted from the Variety Pack and I had cream instead of plain milk and real big strawberries.

Back in Omaha again life continued to be exciting. In winter I trudged very slowly to school, walking in snow up to my waist by choosing the ditches beside the road. Sometimes I'd stop and make a snow angel. It was wonderful. Sometimes I would arrive when it was almost time to dismiss for lunch!

I remember other signs of the Omaha winters with less pleasure—the howling of the storm door in the wind like a wild banshee and the endless yellow capsules of cod liver oil forced down my throat by my mother who insisted that "You can't survive the Omaha winters without them!" I really think that woman believed that!

One day I wandered home for lunch and arrived quite late! Mother said, "Here's your sandwich. Now turn around and eat it on the way back to school. You're very late!

I said, "Oh, Mother, the clouds are so beautiful today!"

It was a very small country school and it was great because of my kindly and encouraging teacher, Mrs. Dinsmore. I was lucky enough to have her for kindergarten, first, and second grades! She kept changing what grade level she was teaching and advanced right along with us.

I was a prolific reader even in kindergarten, sounding out words as I went. I goofed up a few such as "facade" (fack-ade) I thought, and "determined" which became "deter-minded" to me! I read all of the Oz books and all of the Mary Poppins books and every myth and fairy tale I could get my hands on. I remember actually crying when I read the last P.L. Traverse Mary Poppins book and saying, "It's not fair that there aren't any more!"

Mrs. Dinsmore let me read to the class while she did desk work and started by letting me choose what to read. Unfortunately, that ended as the other students weren't really ready for my selections.

In first grade she asked me to try to teach the boys who were behind so we went out in the hall and put our chairs in a reading circle. She did this on the theory that children learn best from other children. I tried to teach them to sound out the words, but the trouble was that they really didn't care about learning and only wanted to talk about other things. They were boring readers about Alice and Jerry and then later Dick and Jane.

Paper was scarce during World War II so we drew our art lesson on the back of the arithmetic page. To this day, I write on both sides of the paper. Mother used to say she could tell which of her daughters wrote to her by looking to see if both sides were used.

My parents were very patriotic as was my teacher so I grew up with tears in my eyes and a big lump in my throat at patriotic celebrations and songs.

One day each week Mother went to some school in Omaha for knitting classes and to assemble boxes to be mailed to our service men.

She took me and my sister along because there were supervised games for the children while the parents learned. Once an older girl asked if she could walk my sister around the block because she was so cute and I said, "Sure."

A little later Mother appeared and had the shock of her life when I told her. I hadn't seen a thing wrong with it. Thankfully we got her back.

We had a morning assembly at school at which we sang patriotic songs and saluted the flag. Whoever looked the most sincere was given first choice of instruments in the school orchestra. (The triangles were the most popular and the blocks were least!) I loved music and stood very straight and tall, always hoping for first pick.

My only other memory of these first grades was getting my mouth washed out with soap, and I still don't remember what I said, but it must have been really bad.

Well, yes, there is more—I shouldn't have said that.

I was in first or second grade when my good friend named Douglas Walker contracted polio the day after his birthday party. I had sat right next to him and my parents were frantic! Fortunately, my angel protected me. Polio was the big fear then and because of it I wasn't allowed in any swimming pools or crowds such as the state fair. All we could do in the boiling hot summers in Omaha was run through the hose, which we did enjoy.

One of my classmates, Ronnie Brodkey, was "Dear Abby's" nephew as I discovered later. That practically made him a celebrity.

Other highlights of living there for me were pony rides (one of my classmates, Jerry Finnecaro, had a pony) and toboggan rides down a steep neighborhood hill.

I remember how kind my parents were—often asking single people to Sunday dinner and then of course singing at the piano with them. We had secretaries from Bozell and Jacobs, newspaper people and sometimes, my godparents, Bess Bozell (who later went to live in Paris. She preferred it to Omaha, I guess) and Ferdinand G. Smola, a Czechoslovakian count. He loved to sing, "Besame Mucho." He told me what it meant—I'd had no idea he was so romantic. We spent some Sundays in lovely Elmwood Park and there are pictures of us, dressed to the nines.

Other Sundays Dad took me to the art museum (Jocelyn Memorial) and my major recollection there was dragging my fingers through the marble golf fish pond in the foyer. I think Dad was letting Mother take a nap. He knew wonderful stories about paintings and artists that I always enjoyed.

When my sister, Debbie, was still a baby, I went over to play with Johnny Agee. My mother was shopping or playing bridge at the time and I told Bernice (the live-in maid) where I was going. The back door was open so

I went in. There were workmen there working on the furnace. I went all over the house looking for Johnny, not knowing that the family had left on vacation. Meanwhile the workmen left, unaware of my presence. I tried all the doors but couldn't open any. (I was about five at the time). Then I went in the kitchen to see how much food there was, so I would figure out how long I could last. After that I walked around the first floor looking for the lowest window. Then I went into the playroom looking for the hardest toy. I then spotted the phone and called, telling the operator what number I wanted. Bernice answered and said that my mother wasn't home. I asked if she could come and get me out somehow and her answer was, "I can't leave the baby." That baby again!  She said that my Mother would be gone for a long time. I panicked and went back to my first plan, thinking I might starve to death before I was rescued. I took the wooden horse and heaved it through the picture window and was free!  Instead of the praise I expected to get for my ingenuity I was in terrible disgrace. My parents never did understand the fear and despair that had gripped me.

Mother who was always very polite was once so aroused that she did a very atypical thing, I thought. A boy in my class, Tommy Morrow, put a rock inside a snowball and hit me in the head with it. Blood came pouring out. Mother took one look and marched me off to his house so his parents could see it in person and how bad it was. She kept saying, "His father is a doctor!" I remember the horrified look on Mrs. Morrow's face.

I still had the wanderlust and ability to get lost. One Halloween I was trick-or-treating with a friend and was out 'til 10:00! The family called my parents who promptly came for me. I had no idea where I was.

My idyllic life changed a bit when I went into third grade. This classroom, on the ground floor held not only third grade but fourth and fifth grades too! One would be reading while the next grade was reciting and the last grade in the room was writing. I don't know how the teacher, Maudeen Stuart, or the students survived. It was also a pivotal year for me because arithmetic was getting harder and I truly hated it. I loved every other subject.

One afternoon my playmate across the street, Linda May, and I were playing a board game on the floor of my parents' bedroom. Two boys were hunting in the cornfield behind my house and a bullet came whizzing in, inches from where I was sitting. Mother was absolutely wild. She called the sheriff and probably

President Roosevelt—I wouldn't doubt it! There was my guardian angel again.

Often Pat and Mike would come to meet me, somehow sensing the time as dogs can, and there they would be as I came out . What a great greeting! One day Mrs. Dinsmore let them come to school but decided it was too disruptive.

My father sent them off to war at one point. Maybe he decided that since he couldn't get in the Navy he would send something off—even just two dogs for the Canine Corp. I was heartbroken but tried to put up a brave front. Imagine my joy when they were returned a short time later due to their friendliness. The soldiers kicked them and tried to toughen them up, but my dogs only licked their boots, so they gave up!

In the middle of third grade my Dad was offered the chance to run one of the branch offices and it just happened to be the one in Indianapolis!  Maybe the guardian angel was trying to unite us with Mother's family.

Mother was an only child and I'm sure the distance was hard on her and her parents. She also had an aunt and uncle in Indy and many friends there. Heretofore her parents had driven out once or twice and we had all been together in Leland, Michigan for part of the summer each year. It was very cool in Northern Michigan but quite a haul from Omaha.

I had one overriding fear—it was of snakes—and sometimes I dreamed about them. I wanted to sleep with the light on, but my parents wouldn't let me. I still think they should have let me have a nightlight. Anyway, when I was about two we were up at Good Harbor, Michigan, where my family went the first year, and a snake crossed the path. Mother shrieked and nabbed me, screaming until her father came and stabbed it repeatedly with a pitchfork. Talk about fears being learned! (It was probably a garter snake, way up there). I'm much better about them now but still fear them.

I really don't blame Mother—she simply couldn't help herself. She was very careful to hide her fear of thunderstorms from me. I've never feared then, and, as an adult, discovered this facet of my Mother. I told her that I'd never seen her looking scared during a storm and she said that it was because she had been under the bed at the time!

# Later Childhood: Indianapolis

Dad went off to take on his new job leaving Mother behind with two children and a house to sell. Dad wrote lots of letters and challenged me to learn to spell "Indianapolis." Sometimes he wrote me my own letters. He explained that we would have to leave our dogs because we would be living in town near the school my Mother wanted us to attend and we would not have an acre of land, just a lot, at the house there. I couldn't imagine what anything smaller would be like, but it didn't sound good.

During this time period Dad called once from Indianapolis. It was night and Mother was across the street playing bridge. Since we only had one phone line (a party line at that!) and I wasn't supposed to leave the baby, I had to figure out how to notify Mom. I told Dad to hang on while I went to the front door and started blinking the outside lights rapidly off and on. (No, I didn't know Morse code). Someone looked up from the bridge table and noticed. Mother said that something must be wrong so over she came. They really praised me for that idea!

We moved to Indy in the middle of the school year sometime and I still remember what I wore to my first day of third grade at Dewitt S. Morgan School #86. The teacher had me stand at the head of the class and introduced me as a new student named Judy Gallup.

"Is that Gallop (G-A-L-L-O-P?)" she asked.

I answered, "No, U-P," and the class dissolved in hysterics. I was mortified. I'm not the only one who remembers that. My old friend Consy, at the age of 60, asked if I remembered and I told her that I would NEVER forget it.

Our new house lacked my wonderful library with the red leather window seat where I read all of my books, but it had another screened in porch and my room was above its roof—handy for escapes. The yard was level except for a steep front bank. Dad told me the right way to pull dandelions and told me he would pay me 50 cents per bushel. I proudly showed him a bushel basket full. He promptly put his big foot in and stomped down and said, "It's NOT full." That still makes me mad.

In school I found I could tell my teacher that we were studying other things in math, back in Omaha, and that's why I was behind. It worked for a while, but Esther Reinke ("Cranky Ranky" we called her) was no fool. I really needed tutoring but kept floundering along.

I enjoyed my new friends very much. There were so many and we were all so compatible! We were all Brownies together and played together every Saturday, all day!

I was an energetic Brownie and then a Girl Scout. We had fun overnights and hikes and our own lingo. We made things to sit on called our "sit-upons" and carried a "walking salad" and we had assigned tasks like "wood gatherers" and "trail blazers." We toasted marshmallows on long sticks over fires we had built and stuffed them in between soft Hershey and graham crackers—probably the first "S'mores" ever. Sometimes we rode horses or went hiking.

My favorites were basketball games you could play as a contest, bike riding and bike tag, bike picnics, swinging down from our flat garage roof on slender saplings growing next to it, calisthenics like back bends and front limbers, cartwheels, dive rolls ,"Tappy on the Ice Box," treasure hunts—anything active, I guess. Sometimes we all went horseback riding or to the Civic Theatre to try out for a role for children. We also all went ice skating at the Coliseum on sparkling colored ice. Two of our group were very good (Consy and

Carolyn) and had little velvet dresses with glittering trim around the hem. Me, I never did very well and never could skate backwards. I did manage to improve a little. Grace was not my specialty!

We were quite creative as a group and made up even a play and actually performed it for our parents in a garage. Susie's parents did hard things like stage lights. They really supported us.

Some Saturdays we went to the Ritz or the Vogue Theater to see the Saturday morning run of endless, mindless cartoons, it's true, plus a serial like "Zorro" or "The Perils of Pauline" and "Movie Tone News."

Other Saturdays we converged for "The Saturday Morning Monopoly Club." Occasionally I would go over to Dottie Dunlap's and we played every single board game she had—quite a stack!

I was never bored with the possible exception of the Saturdays when my friends would sit around making doll clothes from millinery scraps brought home by Susie's father, a milliner. I hated dolls. I also hated sewing—a bad combination.

One girl set up a store in her house and sold school supplies with play money, carefully recording each sale.

I always enjoyed having lots of friends—not one or two—so there was always a pal to be with.

I had one friend who loved basketball and some Saturdays we played competitive games like "Horses" and "Eliminations" for hours on end.

There was a vacant lot at the end of the street—at 49th and Graceland—where we played "Scrub" (three-man version of baseball) and kickball. Once there was a violent cloudburst suddenly and I was soaked to the skin when I got home.

Consy reminded me of our climbing on new house construction escapades and how I once fell through the chimney shaft from the 2nd floor to the basement without touching the sides. Fortunately, there was a pile of soft dirt down there! I had completely forgotten that.

I had another adventure that didn't turn out so well: while roller skating and carrying a friend piggy back, I was tripped up by a crack in the street and went down on my forehead with my friend on top of me. I had blood pouring out of my forehead and was so afraid that I would be scarred for life! My dad, without any hesitation, poured a lot of iodine into it and told me not to touch it or put any bandage over it. I was so worried and so embarrassed to appear in school with that ugly disfiguring scab, but I did. My friends all teased me and make gestures about tearing it off!

All our parents were very supportive, but we took the lead in choosing activities. TV had not reared its ugly head yet, to say nothing of computers, so we were resourceful and learned lessons in leadership and social interaction. (This is one of my preachy platforms!)

Sum total of this childhood in Indianapolis: we were creative, made our own choices, entertained ourselves, read books. We had no electronic distractions! I did like "Let's Pretend" on the radio and "Inner Sanctum" which was scary. And we played those wonderful 45's and all had our own little record players.

# Mother

One day Mother was returning home from shopping and stopped at one of those four-way stops which had been in effect in Indiana for many, many years. She was hit hard by a car that did not stop. She was suddenly headed back in the direction she had just come from and she thought, Wait a minute, didn't I just come from there?

She knew a man who was in his front yard and saw it all and she asked if he would take her side in the matter. He responded that he didn't want to get involved. I was about 10 when she recounted this story and I'm now 80 and I have never forgotten such cowardice. Damn it! Stand up for what's right and be counted! I remember his name, too.

Mother used to say these things about Omaha, which she disliked intensely:

"It takes all the styles one year to cross the Mississippi River from the East!"

(One of the department stores was "The Nebraska Clothing Company" - to give you the idea!)

And my favorite: "Omaha doesn't have anything but weather, and plenty of that!"

# Mrs. Gates' Dancing School

A blur of seamed stockings, faille and taffeta dresses, white gloves and crystal punch bowls passed swiftly in front of me—white gloves, yes, even the boys wore them, bowing at the waist and awkwardly asking me to dance. Endless conga lines on that second floor of the venerable Propylaeum, a fortress of red brick, grey stone and winding porches presiding over "old" Indianapolis since the early 1800's. One of the boys, clowning around, opened a door leading to the fire escape, and the conga line paraded out, everyone laughing. Another boy with pockets full of marbles, rolled them across the wooden floors, causing giggles and tripping feet of the dancers.

I was one of those girls who attained their adult height by the age of 12. Most unfortunately, most of the boys were sawed off runts until many years later, so I wore Capezio velvet flats and slumped a little in order to be their dancing partner. There were two exceptions to this rule, one of whom was a nice, fun guy and the other resembled a block of wood both in personality and looks! (I wonder if he ever learned the art of conversation!)

Next came the line to the punch bowl and being escorted by a gloved companion in the ritual necessary to partake of the sticky lime liquid.

The mothers took turns driving the same group of friends to Mrs. Gates' dancing class each Tuesday. My great Aunt Kate, who considered herself the Emily Post of Indianapolis society, declared firmly that young ladies did not have to attend Tudor Hall School, but they most certainly did have to go to Mrs. Gates.

# An Evening at Home

My parents always had a long cocktail hour during which time I was upstairs studying. I was called to dinner that was always in the formal dining room with Mother in a cocktail dress and Dad in a business suit. I was anxious to share something from my school day with them, but my father would pronounce it "not of general interest" and would discuss how he knocked them dead with his creative ads. (He was vice president and general manager of the Indianapolis office of a large advertising firm). I have to give it to him—he was very successful and had to deal with all kinds of products and the variety of people behind them. He could be very entertaining describing how he "wowed" them. Looking back, I am in awe of how he could sell his ideas for a year's campaign with just a flip chart! He talked about creating a need in people for products. He wrote and illustrated a great ad, showing a woman reading in a wing chair while her "electric servants" worked. (her oven, washer, and dryer). He told funny stories about a client who was a farmer type and head of a feed company who said, "What the 'salesmens need are them in-centatives!'" He got a kick out of bad grammar since he was such an accomplished wordsmith.

I listened politely and then followed Mother into the kitchen to recount the happenings of my school day and my friends' activities because she was always vitally interested.

# Scarlet Fever

My story begins one bright Easter morning in 1947. My little sister and I were decked out in our lovely outfits and shiny new patent leather shoes. My parents had decided to go to the service at St. Paul's Episcopal Church at 62nd and Meridian St. there in Indianapolis. It's quite cathedral-like with yellow stone exterior, high arched entrance, stone floors and of impressive size.

There was no room left to sit down so we stood along the side along with many others. Midway through I started to feel ill and began to shiver. I knew better than to complain, but I felt worse on the ride home and confided in everyone there.

Dad wanted pictures of his family in their Easter finery so we posed in the front yard but I told him how cold I was. He said, "Pretend it's a hot summer day." He snapped away and I still have the picture of me with an unnatural smile, a navy blue light weight coat, my dressy dress, white anklets, with neatly turned down cuffs, a round straw hat with a navy ribbon blowing in the breeze and those patent leather Mary Jane's. My sister, whom I resented for her big dimple and honey blonde curls, stood next to me, beaming and looking like a darling baby doll.

Mother, hovering in the background, sat me down and took my temperature. It must have been high because the next thing I knew I was in bed.

The next day we rode downtown to the doctor. (Back in those days, almost everything important was downtown—doctors, dentists, shopping, everything.)

Both our doctor and our dentist had offices in the important professional building downtown called The Hume Manser Building. (We kids corrupted this to "The Human Sewer Building," of course.)  It was one of our tallest buildings and the elevator took us to the ninth floor to the dentist. I can't remember what floor our physician was on, but he was a very kind, soft-spoken man with wavy gray hair, Dr. Herbert F. Call. His nurse wore one of those pointy, highly starched white nurses' caps held on with bobby pins and she was just as good at her job as he was at his.

Mother was pretty pale and shaky when he diagnosed me as having scarlet fever. She really almost lost it.

He said, "Don't worry, Mrs. Gallup, it's a very light case."

A few minutes later we were back on the elevator. Mother always made us hold our breath on the elevator. Her theory was that there were a lot of sick people on the elevator and if we held our breath we wouldn't inhale their germs. Never mind that we turned blue from the first floor to the ninth and fell out gasping wildly!  I wondered if the other elevator passengers held their breath as we descended—after all I was sick.

Many good things happened to me as I convalesced! I learned to patiently work big detailed jig saw puzzles on a card table across my bed with two legs on the floor; my class mates gave me gifts; my dad brought me a little surprise each day when he came home from work; and since we were quarantined with a big sign on the front door, neighbors volunteered to bring us groceries.

One neighbor decided to negotiate and approached mother with, "If your daughter will stop ringing our doorbell and then hiding and will not take short cuts through our yard, we'll bring you some groceries."

I hated having my parents hear about my badness!

Mother brought me down to the living room couch one day where I could hear some wonderful records on our Stromberg Carlson console record player. I loved Broadway musicals like Oklahoma, Babes in Toyland, and others. My parents had an extensive collection. Mother also brought out some of her favorite books such as one by The Hoosier Poet, James Whitcomb Riley ("Little Orphan Annie Came to Our House to Stay") and, oh, groan, her "Little Colonel" series. I think she had every one. They were so dated they seemed dry as proverbial dust to me, plus The Little Colonel had a strong Southern accent which made her old-fashioned comments almost undecipherable for me! It was a bad combination I simply couldn't overcome and I remember hating to hurt Mother's feelings, but I had to be honest and decline the opportunity to wade through them. I did, however, get the choice to read some books that I did love and memorize nonsense poetry, such as "The Walrus and the Carpenter." Different classmates would deliver my homework to the front steps, ring our doorbell and dart away! I did have to keep up, although some nice allowances were made for poor little sick me!

But the really wonderful, downright heavenly thing to come as a result of my illness was my grandparents' offer to send me to summer camp. You see, I was my adult height of 5'8" but had lost weight and only weighed about 95 pounds! This girls' camp in Wisconsin claimed that girls who needed to lose weight did so while those who needed to gain actually would. My grandparents and parents knew a family who had sent their daughters there and before long we were all getting together. Sure enough, Susan and Connie, the sisters, had loved it there, but were now in their late teens and no longer interested in returning. The upshot was I was to go. Never mind that I didn't know one solitary soul who would be going!

Soon my family and I were invited to a lovely party to introduce prospective campers, their parents, and to show movies of this wonderful place up the north woods! Red canoes bouncing around in the river rapids, smiling girls on cantering horses—wow!  I really wanted to go!

What a wonderful formative experience it was!  My parents were glad that I didn't have any good friends going because they wanted me to make friends and stand on my own feet at the age of 11. How wise!  I have never been shy about meeting people. This stood me in very good stead throughout my entire life and was just the first of many benefits.

I also gained at least ten pounds—maybe more. It was a long time ago and some memories fail! The camp cook was just wonderful. Except for these two summer months, he was a chef at The Waldorf Astoria. What I wouldn't give for his cheese soufflé, vegetable soup, corn pones, and heavenly desserts. (We would raffle off any extra ones by holding up any number of fingers on the shout of "one, two, three horsengoggle!" and then a complicated numbering game ensued that ended in who won dessert.) We had steak and mashed potatoes each Saturday night and waited eagerly for that day to roll around. We always said that if parents were visiting on the weekend, they would think that was how we dined every night!

I remember one instance of sneaking into the main bungalow and putting my initials into the icing of the biggest cupcake so no one else would want it!

The worst devilment, however, was the exchanging salt shakers' and sugar bowls' contents that a friend and I managed to do in one of the dining rooms one night. We enjoyed watching campers squeal and scream in agony as they tasted a very salty cereal!

The sports were such fun and we were so fortunate to have the quality of teaching that we did. Our sense of achievement in this area was measured by awarding us red, blue and gold stars as we fulfilled the requirements in each category. Besides all the fun I had, I acquired a certain level of skill in various sports that was a great confidence builder.

Lifelong friendships came out of my three summers there. In college I talked my roommate into going with me as counselors. So much good came out of having scarlet fever!

# Christmas

No one loved Christmas more than my mother! Some may have loved it as much, but I doubt it.

My sister and I were decorating the big spruce tree in the corner of the den, being careful to hang the icicles around the green fingers of the branches and enjoying reminiscing about each ornament. Many were carefully preserved paper ornaments from the WWII era—soldiers and sailors with shiny silver on the back and brown or blue uniforms on the front.

Suddenly into the room, bursting open the kitchen door, came Mother with punch cups in her hands, singing in her clear alto voice, "We need a little Christmas, right this very minute."

We all joined together in a very happy moment that I'll never forget.

After dinner we would cluster behind the heavy Victorian needlepoint piano bench while Dad played Christmas carols from the beautiful book illustrated by Tasha Tudor and, as he turned the page and we all began to sing the next one, Mother would exclaim, "That's my favorite carol!" and then as the next one came up she would enthusiastically shout, "No, that's my favorite."

I think they all were except perhaps "Good King Wenceslas," I never heard her exclaim over that one.

Mother's cousin Michael, often with Christmas tree ornaments dangling from his pockets, his wife and three lovely daughters would arrive on Christmas Eve, decked out in their best dresses and patent leather shoes, ready to sing carols they had rehearsed in three part harmony. Mother was overjoyed and begged for more!

This was my happy life at Christmas and of course I thought it would last forever.

Then came the exciting part of Christmas Eve with my grandfather (Bopa) playing the role of Santa to the hilt. Seated beside the tree, he read the names on the gift tags as he handed out presents from the huge piles beneath the tree. He did a wonderful job of keeping everyone busy unwrapping at the same time.

The dinner was always perfection itself: the most delightful dishes. from the rarest, most tender roast beef to a selection of homemade pastries and cakes, accompanied with sparkling burgundy. (Whatever happened to that? You can't find it anywhere.)

After dinner we adjourned to the living room and

soon the house was bursting with happy people—friends and neighbors who wanted to come where the party was!

And no wonder—my father played everyone's special favorite song which they sang with him and some danced. Bopa put on a floor show complete with costumes!

Swinging a cane, he became Ted Lewis and asked, "Is everybody happy?"

Then, grabbing a scarf, he put it on his bald head and became Sophie Tucker, belting out in his beautiful baritone, "Some of these days, you're gonna miss me, honey."

He closed with a gorgeous, show-stopping, "If you were the only girl in the world."

You wouldn't hear a sound from anybody in the room.

He then whirled each lady around the floor in turn singing it just to them.

Need I tell you that they loved it?

At the height of the merriment it was time for midnight mass so most of the guests were heading for it, including Bopa. I would be the driver.

The next day Mother would put in a call to the piano tuner as the Steinway survived another rough workout.

One of the guests (Bob Kirby) hammered out Irish tunes on it and really banged them out: "McNamara's Band" seemed to go right along with the carols and Bopa's floor show as most of the guests were Irish!

The piano tuner rates a story of his own. Once when he raised the top of the grand piano he discovered why it didn't sound right! Guests had dropped peanuts and parts of cheese sandwiches down on the strings.

At one time my parents had a blind piano tuner who raised the lid, not knowing that my father had a large antique bottle filled with colored water that resided there. Blam! Splash! He was so apologetic and Mother vainly tried to console him. She flat hated that bottle and was so glad it happened. I asked her how Dad took it. She answered, "He was philosophical."

In 7th or 8th grade we had a terrific teacher, recruited by our parents, named Marie Bagnoli. She was equally adept at teaching all studies and really taught us to think by the questions she would ask, thus she made us understand historic movements such as "nationalism," for instance. She knew how to involve us and pull the answers out of us.

She also taught those of us who were interested how to type, after school on her own time. That led to the formation of a school newspaper in which we were all involved, whether as reporters, news editors, feature editors, or feature story writers. The mothers helped with ancient (not mimeographing) and rudimentary copy machines. At our 60th birthday reunion, Barbara Smith brought a paper she had saved!

I had my first dates with Jon Schmidt. He used to look at my braces and ask how my grill work was coming along! I was so glad to have them as my teeth had stuck out so much that I could hardly close my mouth, but in those days, orthodontists waited until every single permanent tooth was in.

Jon used to ride his bike over to my house and before long we were going to Friday night dances at The Riviera. We went almost every Friday for a while – both loving to dance.

# Shortridge High

High School was also a very fortunate blessing. Shortridge was one of two leading high schools in the Midwest (The other then was New Trier in a Chicago suburb).

Our high school, Shortridge, was very well known for academic excellence and was second only to New Trier, in an affluent Chicago suburb. I was so lucky to be a Shortridge Blue Devil! First of all, the school boasted three paths to learning: vocational education for those not interested in college, Eastern schools, and Indiana colleges. The vocational training included carpentry, mechanics, and printing. Eastern college preparation was more difficult than Indiana colleges and included hearing representatives who visited from some of these schools as well as periodically taking sample SAT's from time to time.

My mother said, "I don't care if you end up at IU or Purdue, you will get a better education on the Eastern track!"

And there I was, at 2:30 when most of my friends were leaving in my hated chemistry lab, getting runs in my stockings from dripping sulfuric acid and sweating under my long black apron.

There were many wonderful experiences as well and in four years there I had outstanding English teachers for my favorite subject—all but one which is pretty amazing—and I took three years of French and two of Latin, which I'll always remember with great happiness. I especially adored Latin and Greek Derivatives, which has been helpful all through life in analyzing word meanings.

We had a daily newspaper with five different complete staffs and I wrote a gossip column with my friend, Ty Schmidek called "Inside Peeks." We also had advanced language classes and many other innovative programs.

Mother never missed an open house and the teachers told her that the parents who came really weren't the ones who should come, usually. Mr. Lett, my algebra I teacher liked me or I'd be there yet. He used to pick his ear with a nail! When Mother asked how I was doing he merely shook his head, and said, "Oh, that Judy." He never elaborated so she really didn't know how I was doing, happily. What got me was the ridiculous word, "simplify," after two brackets of so much confusion with numbers and symbols in them that they looked to me like a war was going on. I thought the only way to simplify that mess was to erase it. Geometry, on the other hand, I understood in general because it says, "If this is true, is this also true?" Now that makes sense to me.

We put on a great show called "The Follies" which was comprised of about five different acts with lots of singing and dancing to tie in with the act's theme. I did a bar stool dance to "Vanessa" in opera hose and heels that was fun.

We had social clubs and I belonged to two or three. And crazy slumber parties – especially at Judy Strohm's – making fudge in the middle of the night – and oh, those little 45's on those colored discs that we played on our portable record players.

At last graduation approached and I and the 243 others in my class were ready for the big ceremony to be held in the huge coliseum at the Indiana State fairgrounds. We were seated alphabetically and I sat watching the families all file in, talking excitedly. I kept scanning the audience for signs of my parents and grandparents! At last they appeared smiling, talking, and looking around to see if any seats were left at the late hour.

I saw Mother smile and point and say, "Oh, look! There are 7 or 8 seats in a row!"

They headed in that direction and sat down, looking pleased. The next thing that happened was a huge American flag unrolled from the distant rafters above, landing in their laps and completely obscuring their faces and bodies! You never saw such a scurrying in your life! The stars and stripes were fluttering wildly!

# College

Having gone to a large coed high school in the Midwest, I thought my college experience should be entirely different so that I could learn more. I thought a women's college (with a male or coed college nearby) either in the East or the South, would be a good choice. I particularly liked the idea of studying during the week and then partying on the weekend – and if you knew the answer to a question you didn't have to hang back because you might look like a know-it-all to the boys in your class.

In those days of no computers, colleges employed traveling representatives to show pictures of their schools to high school students.

On such slender bodies of evidence hung my whole life when I took one look at the graceful columns on the cream-colored Mary Baldwin College buildings and declared, "I want to go there!"

After all, hadn't I laid the foundation for such a choice by choosing to go to Camp Bryn alone by myself six years earlier? The building blocks of life do have meaning.

I spent the summer having one last fling with my high school buddies and studying French quite seriously. Mother couldn't understand why I was doing that so I explained that I really wanted to study English literature in college and if I passed a difficult French entrance exam I would be allowed to take a conversational advanced French course focusing on poetry and plays instead of grammar and after one year I wouldn't need any more foreign languages and could start taking more English courses.

At last the great day to go off to college arrived. Mother had taken me shopping for a new wardrobe and off I went in a lovely brown plaid suit, brown leather Capezio stacked heels, brown cashmere hat, a six pack under one arm and my ukulele case under the other! I stepped on the platform and into the Pullman car where my roomette was. Lo and behold there were about six other girls on that train heading for Staunton, Virginia – girls who had left their homes in Texas two days prior! The train had taken them north to Chicago and finally started East through Indianapolis! They were very glad to see me with a six pack of Miller beer and I made friends easily! As it turned out, they were some of my very best college friends. I find Texans to be a lot of fun and had already met a few at camp.

I was quite happy and excited and loved spending the night on the train. The roomette was small and you either had a bed or a seat – you had to choose!

We chugged into the most beautiful mountain scenery – it was actually my first look at mountains and I was enchanted by their beauty!

At the station we were met by older girls from the college – our "big sisters," who were there to make us feel welcomed and to show us around. They had name tags on their pretty plaid dresses.

I settled into my dorm very happily with some strong boys heaving my black steamer trunk behind me.

Thus began a four-year adventure filled with dear friendships, wonderful professors and fascinating studies, the chance to sing in glee club and chapel choir and trips as members of these groups, weekends at U. Va. and Washington and Lee, class trips and Washington, DC, and New York--so much fun!

If I hadn't gone to Mary Baldwin I wouldn't have met my future husband and become the mother of a wonderful daughter!

My roommate was one of those fun Texan girls from the train, which was terrific. In those days we corresponded with the school before arriving about what our preferences in roommates was and I had asked for a Texan and got, Janey from Galveston, cool! She confessed to me later that she had requested someone from New England, feeling that it would be cool to know someone very sophisticated – and what did she draw! Plain old me - "corn off the Indiana cob" and even more unsophisticated, originally a Nebraska cornhusker!

Janey was not much of a student, but she was a lot of fun, pretty, and a dreamer. She liked to play Jackie Gleason's LP called "Music to Make You Misty" and lie on the bed and stare into space.

I went to the library a lot because I didn't want to waste my parents' money and because I really liked to study hard during the week, make good grades, and party on weekends. That framework suited me perfectly and I was so pleased with my courses and the professors!

We had a choice between math or biology so I opted for the latter, being a math phobe all my life.

I tried to stay awake in botany, but for me it was a real sleeper. Our professor, Dr. Humphreys, had great faith in our class, so I really studied leaves and trees as diligently as possible so as to not let her down.

Second semester brought forth biology with rats to cut open. We each got one. I can still remember that awful formaldehyde acrid odor and my intense dislike of cutting into my rat.

Our professor got so excited because someone got a pregnant rat! To me it was more reason to feel sick.

I remember thinking it would be hilarious to cut off the tail and tie it to the dangling light cord in our dorm room and watch Janey turn it on. It was very funny, all right!

On Sundays we were required to attend the church of our choice and the four of us who were Episcopalians (three Texans and I) marched off in our hats and gloves carrying our prayer books. We had a Methodist and a Southern Baptist Texan as well.

One day we rebelled and hid in our closets when the college officers came around to do a room check.

That wasn't our only idea for hiding in the closets. We had some aged bourbon in one of the hat boxes.

Speaking of bourbon, the college had a strict rule that we couldn't drink within a 50-mile radius. One night I went to our party place, Crafton's, which was an old log cabin in the country with a fireplace and different musical groups – so we would dance there.

I decided to have one beer one night because, of course, my date was having beer. Word somehow got around and I was hauled before the Judiciary Council made up of my peers (my very strict peers) and I was thoroughly grilled. I escaped expulsion by the skin of my teeth!

I loved the fraternity parties on weekends and definitely preferred W & L to U.Va. because no matter how hard they partied boys from W & L always remembered that you were their date and treated you well and I can't say that for the U.Va. crowd I knew.

One night at the Phi Kappa House (Phi Kappa Psi) they dipped one of the boys' feet in a bucket of tar or black paint, held him upside down, and had him make footprints across the ceiling. That may have been the same night when I decided my girdle was too tight so I left it in the ladies' room on a table. Of course, I forgot it and of course my mother had stamped my name in it in huge black capital letters and of course it was thumb tacked onto a bulletin board in the house for all to see. I begged one of them to get it back of me!  If anyone can think of anything that embarrassing, I'd love to hear about it!

The Phi Gams had a terrific party with about 6" of beer you waded through in the basement so of course everybody was barefoot. They were serving everything, of course, so I thought I'd have a martini. (I had never had one). It was a small drink so I thought you were supposed to chug it. The room started spinning, I can tell you.

One boy there was known as "The Snow King" because he "snowed" all the girls with his good looks and Southern charm. He was a campus king from Charleston, South Carolina I was pinned to him for a while, but he was such a flaming flirt that it was a very short engagement!

We often partied very hard on Saturday and stayed in the Mayflower Hotel where the manager was very strict about what time we signed in. Then we gossiped and stayed up even later, chattering among ourselves upstairs.

Sunday came and the only cure for Saturday's revelries were the milk punch parties in the fraternities on Sunday morning where we had plenty of "the hair of the dog that bit us" in the punch – it was mostly gin, rum, bourbon and scotch as I remember (who can really remember) with a blob of vanilla ice cream on top.

Then the boys had to drive us 39 miles back to Mary Baldwin on a three-lane highway! That is only the most dangerous type of highway there is.

One time I came back from an rip-roaring party and went into the main building at school to sign in. The lady who was on duty to oversee this was very nice and she said, "Judy, go right straight to your dorm room and don't talk to anybody!"

Somehow, I made it through four years in that church-affiliated college! ("I get by with a little help from my friends." I see where the Beatles got their title!)

On the scholastic side, I romped through my English lit class with sheer joy!

I loved Chaucer with Dr. Locke who came in the classroom, went to his desk in front and expertly sailed his green velour hat with the small feather over all of our heads to the window ledge behind us. I can still quote parts of Chaucer's Canterbury Tales beginning with, "When that Aprille with its shoures soote."

Dr. Brice taught English Romantic Poets was so old and winkled that it seemed such a contrast, but he obviously loved them so – and I did also! It instilled in me a great hunger for The Lake Country.

Of course, we started it all with Beowulf and we called our professor "Grendel's Mother" due to her looks. Somehow this epic seems to be where everyone starts and such a violent beginning!

Looking back, it seems unbelievable that we got to know our professors so well in that small college of about 325 students. They were so available for questions and would stroll into the club where we were playing bridge or playing instruments. (We formed a group called The Baldwin Bombshells and I played the uke.) The girls seemed to enjoy our efforts and we had a lot of fun playing. Our pianist, Linda L., was one of the Texas group and she played for her church at home. It fascinated me that she went on to play jazz in nightclubs later in life when my recollection of her was a strict Methodist who studied classical piano. The guitarist was another Texan, "M.L.," and she was good – particularly on country ballads – she ended up as a psychologist in Australia!

One year as Christmas approached I was lucky to snag a ride home with a boy from Indianapolis who was a student at Washington & Lee. He had two others with him – his girlfriend and a French student who couldn't make it home to Alsace – Lorraine and his town of Nancy for Christmas. We had a jolly foursome driving through snow and stopping for a lovely lunch at The Greenbrier resort in West Virginia. In those days, their lunch consisted of an endless buffet of every kind of seafood plus choice meats and some tables laden with elegant pastries. Ice sculptures formed huge centerpieces on each linen covered table. We wanted to show America to our French traveler!  His name was Jean-Marie Grandpierre and many people in America, not knowing French, thought it was a girl's name so he had many mix-ups. He had traveled to W & L because he was fascinated by the Civil War and was a history major so a college in the Shenandoah Valley of Virginia was his dream!  We hit it off, what with my three years of French, and he was very handsome and such a kind, real person – not a phony or narcissistic bone in his body!  No one can resist such a thoughtful person I'm sure. We ended up dating for several years and when he graduated I made a trip to see him as he served in the French Navy in D.C. at The French Embassy. He and his companions looked like dolls in those French uniforms – round white hats with a pom pom in the middle!  Nothing like The American Navy uniforms!

I finally broke it off for several reasons. All during this time I had no idea that my parents were holding their breath – they were so afraid I would move to France!

My senior year was marked by the fearsome prospect of written and oral exams in English literature, necessary in order to obtain my B.A.  I studied very diligently, going back over four years of class notes as well as the text books. The footnotes didn't even escape my gaze!

Socially, I was going out with two different boys on the weekends and one was in JAG (Judge Advocate General) school at U.Va. which intrigued me. Their dances were a step above the usual frat dances.

The other boy was an SAE from U.Va., had a thick Southern drawl, and really enjoyed his beer.

A friend from Mary Baldwin kept pestering me about going out with her and her boyfriend and their friend, a "townie" who had gone to U.Va. and then several other universities to get his degree in orthodontics. He was newly arrived back in town to open his practice and everyone thought it would just be dandy if we double dated.

I explained to my Mary Baldwin friend that I was quite busy studying and going out on weekends, plus I did NOT want a blind date.

The third time she pursued the subject I said, "All right then, if you and your date come, I will go."

And that's how I met my husband, the father of my sweet daughter. We went to a U.Va. football game when we double dated. My Mary Baldwin friend, Ruth, joked about being hard up for a date since we were going out with "townies."

We talked all the way to Charlottesville and started down the steep stadium steps. I couldn't believe it –

our seats were all the way down on the front row! We were practically on the field!

My date was completely wrapped up in the game. He would leap to his feet, yelling, cussing, cheering, etc. and then sit back down on his green velour hat. I thought he was crazy or close to it. I have no recollection of who won or what the score was because the entertainment was NOT down on the field.

Afterwards we went to several fraternity houses for beer and more beer. Ruth's date was very entertaining with funny jokes and stories, but my date was mad about losing the game. I thought Ruth's date was fine, but when it was time to get up, he couldn't. He sure could talk, but he sure couldn't walk!

I bid my date a polite "good bye" back at Mary Baldwin and was happy to be back.

I believe it was the very next day that he called. He wanted to go to a movie—and so it began.

I had to study more than he would have liked because he was just starting his orthodontic practice so he had plenty of free time.

Fall marched into winter and we went to more games and on Sundays I often had dinner at his family's home high on a hill overlooking Staunton and the Blue Ridge Mountains. My future mother-in-law even had a telescope positioned by the dining room window from which she could see cars on Afton Mountain. There was a stone near the garage that said it was the highest point in Staunton. The home was named "Four View" and they had built it. I particularly liked to hear the Staunton Military Academy Marching Band play the music – the music drifted right up to the house.

When Ed (my date's name) told his mother that we were going to get married, he told me that she gasped, "You're kidding, aren't you?" Actually, she really liked me and we got along very well. It was just her way of talking.

We drove out to Indianapolis on spring break so Ed could meet my family and I managed to get a speeding ticket on Old Rt. 40 in Ohio.

We made plans to have the wedding June 28, three weeks after my graduation.

My senior year was fast approaching and it was time to start planning the graduation ceremony. Back in the 50's we enjoyed dressing up for formal occasions and even owned hoop skirts with stiff round crinolines underneath to make them stand out.

We decked ourselves in beautiful long white dresses with hoop skirts, long white gloves and carried flowers as we paraded down the steep steps of the back campus. Each of us had two underclassmen who were our "attendants." Our parents and grandparents were seated in folding chairs beside the steps and what an appreciative audience! Interestingly, we had a cold snap in early June and my mother, who thought she was going South, had no warm coat so she had to march down to Schwarzschild's, the women's dress shop, and buy one.

It was a beautiful ceremony and it was so memorable for us all.

It was an important trip for my relatives for other reasons, as they were going to meet their new family members, my fiancé's parents.

During that weekend we had several dinners together and everyone had a great time. My grandfather was such a character and Dr. Armstrong took a very strong liking to him (as everyone in the world did!) and he started showing him his treasured rifle from Civil War days named "Old Betsy" and regaling him with its history. Bopa (my grandfather) wouldn't have known which end to put against his chest and where the bullet came out, but he played right along with him and they were friends for life!

Later they emerged from the kitchen, bourbons in hands, and Dr. Armstrong declared that he and Bopa decided that Virginia Gentleman and Jim Beam came from the same distillery! (Jim Beam was the brand my grandfather represented – he had been President of National Liquors and a Jim Beam distillery.)

My mother-in-law had hired a caterer to cook dinner and it was just lovely. Before that she sat and drank a very watered-down version of a highball as fast as she could. She always reminded me of someone who had to take medicine and it was a grim procedure.

I don't know how my Mother did it, but she managed to pull off a wedding with 400 guests three weeks after graduation!

I helped with what I could, but I remember being baffled when it came to the subject of wedding music, flowers and other necessary details of which I had absolutely no knowledge.

Standing in the back of the church and waiting for the production to start, one of the groomsmen asked if I was ready. I answered in the affirmative. Not all of the wedding party was assembled in the foyer yet. Thinking I was just waiting for the carpet to be unrolled all the way to the foyer and the wedding march to start, the signal was given—all without the cast of characters being ready to march up the aisle!

During the ceremony when the minister asked, "Who

gives this woman?" I heard a loud sniff emanating from my Father before he intoned, "Her Mother and I do" and I was so surprised!  I had no idea at all that he could be so emotional towards me.

I had seen him cry once in my life and it was when a dear friend was killed in World War II. I came down to breakfast watching him cry as he squeezed the orange juice.

The second boo-boo occurred out of sight at the reception. In the kitchen, someone dropped the huge, multi-layered wedding cake and, while the cake itself wasn't hurt, it listed to one side a bit!  It was rather seasick in appearance.

Ed was neurotic about his things—especially his cars. Well, he had a new black Oldsmobile '98 and he was terrified that someone would cover it with whipped cream and write all over it, so he had it parked in a downtown garage near the IAC (Indianapolis Athletic Club) where we had the reception and had one of the groomsmen check on it. No one else knew where it was. He wanted us to sneak away from the reception before anyone followed us throwing rice because they might mess up the car. Seriously!  So we took an elevator and escaped.

When the guests figured out what we had done, they

just threw rice at each other!

Off we drove into the unknown—the start of a new life together! We went to a lovely hotel in Louisville and I remember a wonderful dinner and dancing to a great band that night.

We left the next day for a town in North Carolina. It was not only our destination for a motel but we were also to have dinner with another orthodontist and his wife who lived there. He (Jack) was a great friend of Ed's, so we had a good visit and I liked his wife, too.

The next morning we were heading for our destination of Sea Island, Georgia, the Cloisters. My cousin Mike and his bride had honeymooned there as well as several others I knew and all found it to be idyllic. I would agree with their assessment. I made a big mistake, though! The first day we played golf and I really got sunburned. I had never before gotten a burn- only a deep tan, but I had never been South before! I didn't realize how much closer to the Equator I was.

We honeymooners posed for a group picture on the lawn – it was a bright June day and we all had lovely sundresses and neat sports clothes for the men. It as a beautiful big group and a picture to treasure.

The swimming pools were lovely and had glass walls around then to prevent the wind from coming in where we were sunbathing.

After a few days my new husband became restless and wanted to go back to work and get home! I was in no hurry to set up housekeeping, especially because I knew nothing about it – neither cooking nor cleaning! I'd had this lovely liberal arts education, but I knew nothing about domestic chores. Perhaps that was typical of the 50's unless you lived on a farm.

When we arrived in Staunton several days ahead of schedule, my in-laws were surprised to see us.

Once we settled in our little apartment, my mother-in-law sent dinner over in a big basket, delivered by her other son. What a blessing! This went on for several weeks.

I did have a neighbor in the apartments who realized my predicament so she invited us for dinner, which was pizza out of a box, but she wanted me to come early so I could learn how to make it. That was a lifesaver! She said, "If you make holes in the dough you can always go back and patch them up." So that gave me confidence.

To be fair to me, though, I had a tiny stove and refrigerator in that narrow little kitchen and it was hard to be efficient. There was one ice cube tray so you could either have ice or a frozen salad or dessert.

# Married Life

Settling into married life meant learning what was expected of young ladies in the South in the 1950's and early 1960's. This meant learning the fine art of flower arranging that bored me to death, bridge and dinner parties (which I enjoyed), and learning to play golf. I already loved playing tennis. After a year of this I was pretty restless and just then I was asked to teach English at Stuart Hall, a girl's prep school in Staunton.

I spent a very enjoyable year teaching a subject I loved and was given full latitude to create class projects. I really loved watching the young girls develop their skills with language. In the early 60's in a private school I was able to create many exercises for their young minds such as asking them each to write an autobiography. It's almost laughable—how much living had they experienced by the age of 15, after all? There were moans and deep sighs, but it was a great exercise in writing and I always felt that they needed that for many reasons—not just content but of course grammar and punctuation. (Several thanked me when they were adults that was very rewarding to me).

Another exercise was this: I explained that they were each to go to the board and I would write a verb above their heads (such as "walk") and they were each to write as many synonyms under it as they could, as fast as possible, and we would see who won. I also forced them to read Tom Sawyer and Huckleberry Finn when I discovered their lack of familiarity with Mark Twain. Several girls whined that they were boy's books and that they therefore had no interest in them. I took no pity on them and was rewarded when they admitted that they loved those books!

The bright side of teaching was wonderful, but, as with any joy, there were objectionable elements as follows:

1. We had to attend meetings that were always scheduled on Friday nights! Not only that, much of the meeting was devoted to boarding school problems that had nothing to do with academic life!

2. The Headmistress liked to drop in, unannounced, on random Monday mornings, take a seat in my classroom, and stare at me during most of the lesson, in order to see if I was prepared after my riotous weekend in Staunton, VA.

3. The Headmistress reserved the Supreme Right to read and correct, if necessary, any of my exams

before I gave them. I, of course, will never forget the one correction that was of my spelling for the work, "judgement." She said, "The preferred spelling is judgment." (She was right, but after all, does one have to conform to what's "preferred"?" (Who prefers it?)

My voyage into academia was cut short for several reasons, among them having to teach Saturday classes for a half-day and the almost impossible task of getting a substitute and being excused for any time off. It was a great year in many ways and gave me the ability to stand in front of people and talk which had been impossible for me to think of before that time.

After 17 years, I discovered that my husband and I had irreconcilable differences. I prayed over the matter and decided that the only course of action was to end the marriage and become a realtor since my teaching credentials had long since expired and real estate had always interested me.

There were many other adventures along the way.

# My Guardian Angel Is Here!

One evening I was reading the Wall Street Journal and a large ad caught my attention. It showed about 10 men in business suits carrying brief cases and climbing different sizes of ladders up to a gym and it stated, "On your climb up the business ladder, don't leave your health behind." It was advertising the health clinic at the Arizona Biltmore in Phoenix. I thought it quite clever (my father had taught me something about ads!) until I realized that there were no women in it! Having recently returned from a NAFE (National Association of Female Executives) convention in New York I was even more acutely aware of the absence than usual, so I decided to write the people at that health club a letter.

The next day I laboriously typed a letter at the real estate office (this was before we had computers) and I was careful not to have a feisty tone but rather a helpful one. I quoted the numbers of female executives and said that I felt they were missing quite a large target market.

When I was having dinner a few nights later my phone rang and an executive from the Arizona Biltmore

Health Clinic invited me out there as their guest to have a health exam. Wow! I was thrilled. I asked when I could come and they said that any time was fine. I already knew that the Human Resources people from my China trip had a convention in Phoenix so I timed my trip with that.

I was so happy when the time arrived and was looking forward to being the guest of the Health Clinic at golf and a lovely luncheon at the Velvet Turtle (very chic at the time!) and the tour they gave me, but of course the health exam was drawing near, so I resigned myself and headed to the building.

I was seated with several others and given a tee shirt and jogging outfit with their logo, and had to fill out a questionnaire next.

One question regarded coughing and I answered that I did cough but only in the mornings. Then I handed in the paper and started going through a very thorough exam. The part that will always be vivid in my memory was the underwater weighing. I sat in a huge scale which was lowered into a tank of water and instead of holding my breath before it went under water, I was supposed to exhale completely and then be lowered under water in order to weigh what percentage of my total weigh was muscle and, sadly, what percent was fat. I tried three times before I was successful!  It's not easy.

Then I met with the resident doctor who showed me an ex-ray that they had taken there of my lungs. I stared at it and asked what all those little cul-de-sacs were in them and he answered, "Those are the beginnings of emphysema."  He went on to say that if I quit smoking right now I would be completely clear in about 15 months but that I might want to enjoy my vacation and quit when I got home. I threw my cigarette pack across the room and never had another puff. That was 33 years ago.

Things happen for a reason!  I truly know that God has guided me all through life. (I had never ever typed a letter before or since!)

# Cancer

## My Guardian Angel Speaks Again!

It was a sparkling Sunday at Goshen Pass! My daughter Debbie and I decided to have a peaceful, uplifting Sunday morning perched on a big flat rock with the Sunday papers and swirling rapids around us, just drinking in the glory of unspoiled nature. (This had been a great recreational paradise back in my youth, dating at W & L, and bringing a bottle out there and leaping from rock to rock without spilling it.)

So, reliving my colorful past, I was seated on a rock reading the paper and enjoying the swirling eddies around my rock, when suddenly I spied a snake headed straight for me. The snake had a triangular head and didn't seem a bit scared of the girls splashing in the water near my rock. As far as I was concerned, these were two very bad signs.

I shouted something to Debbie and scrambled down from my perch and headed for the shore as fast as I could run and splash. Reaching the shore I started to break into a run, but a vine growing in the bank wrapped around my ankle and pulled me down. Somehow I fractured one of my ankles so Debbie drove me to the Emergency Room. I recall a lady who was the MD on duty staring at me very coldly as I lay on the examining table and somehow my ankle got x-rayed and wrapped. Instead of kindness the vibe I got was anger that I had disturbed her Sunday! My daughter drove me home in bandages and I made arrangements to be driven to the real estate office in the morning.

Debbie said that she imagined that I would want to postpone my mammogram in Charlottesville at Martha Jefferson until I could drive myself but I said, "No! It's been exactly a year and it's time for me to get it so I'll get there! Debbie made arrangements then and drove me to my appointment.

What a fortunate decision!

I remember Jan and Ann, the very nice X-ray technicians saying, "let me take one more." I awaited the results and they came in and said that we would go down the hall and speak to Mary Beth. This was puzzling but we did as instructed and Mary Beth told us gently that there was breast cancer there but in the very early stages so we could knock it out! I was stunned!

I said, "Well, what do I do? I want to start on the

path of getting rid of it right away! Now!"

She explained about first planning for the surgery and after that treatment with chemotherapy, followed by radiation, and then taking an oral chemotherapy pill every day for five years and not missing a day! (Back then it was tamoxifen).

I asked if we could try radiation first and then, if it worked, I wouldn't need chemotherapy? She explained that it couldn't be done like that. I was diagnosed with "stage one breast cancer," but it was possible that it had escaped the margin and gone into "stage two," so we had to be sure we killed it all! That meant, in my case, three months with one chemo treatment each month.

I was so glad to have Debbie with me as the words sank in.

We walked down that L-O-N-G hall with heavy steps, but both of our friends from mammography took that long walk with us. They asked who my surgeon was and when I told them they said, "Oh, we've heard of him. We've seen some of his results." I said, "Well, that's really damning him with faint praise. Now, as a realtor I know you can't recommend anybody (I can't either) but pretend that I'm your mother. Now, where would you send your mother?"

They answered, "It's so hot today – but then it is summer! It's Summer!

I said, "Oh, Linda Sommers! Thank you so much!"

I gave Dr. Linda Sommers a call.

What a wonderful, caring surgeon she was! We scheduled a lumpectomy at Martha Jefferson Hospital and, lo and behold, she personally wheeled me to the operating room, reassuring me all the way. After surgery I awoke to a huge bouquet of flowers from her! Imagine!

A few days later I went to see her again. Pulling her stool right next to me she explained that we didn't quite get it all and so needed one more lumpectomy. I trusted her completely and the second time we got every bit of it!

Since the doctors assured me that chemo must be done next I girded myself and marched off for my first treatment. A very nice lady from my real estate firm insisted on accompanying me which was one of those acts of kindness that one never forgets. I sat in a large, sun-filled room with several others and received the injection in the top of my left hand. I read and chatted with my friend until it was over. I can't remember if it took 30 minutes or an hour, but it was something in that neighborhood. After the procedure I headed home to rest. Although it took me two days to begin to feel better after each treatment, I found that I could make phone calls from home and my assistant held the office together beautifully. This went on for several months through the fall and early winter. People have said that they didn't know how I kept working, but it was my work and an attempt at normalcy that brought me through it! My oncologist and his entire group were wonderful and kept in touch.

I had a harrowing incident at one point: The staff said that I needed to jump my white blood cell production so I was given neupogen. At 6 AM I awakened the next day with unbelievable pain (seizures in my back) and had to go to the hospital in an ambulance. They took me to ER and started working on me, fearing a heart attack. I called my daughter, a med student in Richmond, and she started driving the 100 miles to help her mother! They wanted to put me in that terrible cylindrical machine where you get claustrophobia and the ER nurse said that it couldn't wait and that she was speaking for Debbie to say that I must go in that MRI scan thing now! Just then daughter, Debbie materialized, smiled, hugged me and held my toes while I was in that fearsome tube listening to the loud rat-tat-tat noise it made.

Happily, my heart was fine, but they had to eliminate the worst case first. They were quite puzzled until one of the fine oncology staff asked me about my chemo treatment the preceding day and I remembered the neupogen shot. He asked what time I'd had it which made perfect sense with what time I awoke with the severe pain. Now I know that I can't tolerate neupogen!

Suddenly it was time to have the radiation treatments! Here it was the dead of winter, and I was slated to drive to Charlottesville every week day for several weeks to be treated. Thank goodness I had a great SUV well up to the task, a Nissan Pathfinder. I remember whizzing by people mired in snowbanks and skidding on the 250 by-pass while I was patting the dashboard and being so grateful for its agility. I absolutely, positively had to keep on schedule with my treatments!

You must believe me here! The radiologist, Dr. Sylvia Hendrix, was so great and had such a sparkling wit and sense of humor that I looked forward to my treatments. Besides, there were often treats for the patients as well as chair massages. I had complete confidence in her, baked her some brownies at Christmas time, and my treatments went well.

# Finding the Gallups

Is there any place as cold, austere and uninviting in this world as a doctor's examining room?  The chill from the table where I waited sent knives into my whole body under the paper cover with which I vainly tried to cover my shaking limbs. I regretted that I left my book in the waiting room. My eyes wandered around the four walls. What was there of any interest?  Wait!  What was that?  Some nice person had donated money to the hospital to honor the memory of a loved one. Let's see—who was it?  Why that's my name!  My maiden name—I had no idea any Gallups were in Virginia!  I'd lived there for 45 years and never once seen my name in print!  Who in the world was Marian Flood Gallup?  My curiosity wasn't just piqued—it was running an amok!

After my appointment with the radiologist I grabbed the Charlottesville phone book and her name was still there!  Now what?  With trembling fingers I dialed and explained who I was. A sweet lady on the other end advised me to call Dr. David Gallup in Crozet who she said knew all about the family. I thought, Why not?

This could be interesting.

This call led to an instant invitation to visit along with directions to his house. Soon I was on my way! I stopped at the little country store and then proceeded. Presently I pulled up in front of a neat brick ranch with a breathtaking view of the purple mountain backdrop.

I knocked and was warmly greeted by Dr. Gallup and his wife, Padma. Dr. Gallup told me that he was a retired congregational minister who had served in India, where he met the lovely dark haired lady who was his wife.

We were seated in the living room, flooded by sunlight, and he began to tell me the story of my family.

He said, "Wait a minute—I'll get the 'red book.' It's all in that."

In a minute he reappeared in the doorway to the adjoining room with a large book bound in red leather. We sat down together and he went over the introduction. It was a thrilling account of Captain John Gallup who set sail from Dorset, England bound for the new world. When he arrived in Boston in 1630, after a long, perilous voyage, he began to immediately help his best friend Governor Winthrop by devising trade routes along the coastline. He stored provisions on Gallup Island, still known by that name, one of many islands in the Boston Harbor. He lived nearby on a generous land grant from the King.

Two more compelling stories were included in this chapter: one about the sails flapping on another ship and Captain Gallup realizing it belonged to his good friend, John Oldham. To his horror he saw pirates on deck so he proceeded to ram the boat repeatedly and then jump aboard and kill and wound the pirates. Climbing below he discovered the corpse of his friend who had been brutally murdered, his head chopped off!

Another tale that caught my interest immediately was the true account of Governor Winthrop's imploring John to get his wife and family here. John was very unhappy without them and had been here for several years but his wife was very reluctant to leave hearth and home in her village.

Winthrop's stirring quote was, "I marvel at the woman's weakness."

He then threatened to withhold John's wages so she finally assented, or I wouldn't be here. All Gallups are related and we sprang from John and his wife.

After this vivid introduction, Dr. Gallup asked me my father's and grandfather's names. He then turned pages in the red book until he found them. I was amazed. To be caught up in this living history was overwhelming.

Dr. Gallup told me that the Gallup Family Association was very active and were about to celebrate their 100th Anniversary and asked if I would like to attend the meeting and celebration! (This was back in 2001).

By then there was no turning back. I was just overwhelmed to be a part of this story.

I drove clear up to Ledyard, Connecticut, where the affair was to take place on the 300 acre family estate (on Gallup Hill Rd., past Gallup School!).

Entering the long drive, I parked near the pool among many other cars and made my way to the huge white house on the crest of the hill. One attendee had a van full of Gallup memorabilia from mugs to pens to stationary to tennis shirts and tees. He said he was in that type of business so it was easy for him. He did a brisk business!

Walking up the white gravel drive past the ever present stone walls I reached the large canvas tent spread over the lush lawn and took a seat on a folding chair next to a long table laden with food and an enormous sheet cake with the number "100" on it.

The program began with a DAR lady in Pilgrim costume who gave an inspiring talk about those Puritan Gallups of long ago. They fought valiantly for their new country even before the Revolutionary War in the Pequot Indian War. Two were Colonels in the Revolutionary War and are buried in the beautiful, peaceful family cemetery on the estate with American Flags next to their headstones.

The cemetery was the most awe-inspiring, peaceful resting place I have ever seen, with ancient trees enclosing the ancient tombstones. Trees that were there many centuries ago covered us in deep shadows. The stone walls and iron gates were beautiful and added to the majesty of the scene.

After lunch we were entertained by little Gallup children who knew their parts perfectly and did The Fife and Drum routines, dressed in Colonial costume.

The next item on the agenda after the business meeting involved all of us finding which people in attendance we were most closely related to and having our picture taken standing between them!  A young fellow, one of the many Roger Gallup's, helped me by systematically identifying my nearest attending relatives in the red book according to a numeric code listed with each name. When they took my picture it was what I call "a life event" for me! I was standing between my nearest relatives in attendance. We all had Gallup Family Tree charts over our heads so you could clearly see the descending line of ancestors we had in common and just where they diverged.

Those who desired could then go swimming in the beautiful pool carved from the rock in the farm soil!  I kept thinking that I was swimming in my gene pool!

The next day I decided to tour Foxwoods, the famous gambling casino nearby. A receptionist greeting me in the impressive entrance hall and asked me about myself.

I explained why I was there and he asked, "Are you a Gallup?"  I answered in the affirmative, so he said, "I'll show you where the whales gambol"!  So I got my own private tour!  It was amazing to me to learn how revered my family is in the Ledyard-Mystic area!

# Surely I'm the Luckiest Person on Earth!

I just returned from an amazing weekend that ranks right up there with what I call my "Life Events!" It was called, innocently enough, "The Spring Fly Fishing Fling" and put on by Martha Jefferson Hospital in Charlottesville. The invitation mentioned that it was for cancer survivors and included fishing and gourmet meals.

When I called to accept I asked how much it would be. I was told that it was free and I could hardly believe it! I have always been interested in fishing so I accepted on the spot.

The next post contained a letter enclosing various waivers of liability, of course, AND a list of suggestions as to what to bring. Upon reading it I was filled with trepidation and wondering what I had done when the first items were "bug spray" and "flashlight"! I could see myself struggling down a path to a one-holer in the middle of the night. Also on the list were "woolen hat," "warm gloves," and "change of clothes". Oh, great—in case I survived a fall in the river I would need them, I supposed.

A long, long, long drive way back in the sticks, up a steep hill, past two tennis courts overgrown with weeds, I finally came to an abrupt stop in a gravel parking lot above a wooden lodge with a glassy lake about 30 steps below it. Other women were pulling up and we exchanged nervous smiles and began making our unsteady way down the steep path. Pulling open the heavy wooden doors we stepped into a timber-lined lodge with rough-hewn beams across the vaulted ceiling. We stood in a great room with kitchen and rest rooms at the far end, and next to us an oversized fireplace big enough to walk in (or roast a bear) that was already filled with gigantic logs making crackling sounds.

We 12 pilgrims were warmly welcomed and given colorful name tags, bandanas, and bright necklaces comprised of different colored inch long fish in a row encircling our necks. We sat in a semi circle in front of the warm hissing and crackling fire, and listened to Mark, our main host, describe the activities for the weekend.

We then went onto the deck outside overlooking the tranquil water below and enjoyed local wines and trays of hors d'oeuvres. We were eager to meet each other and ask about them, their families, and how long they had been cancer-free. As you can imagine, there was never a lull in the conversation, with 12 women.

After about an hour we went back inside and were told by our host that we had, as we were women, always waited on others in our families doing all the necessary household chores, but now we were to be waited on by the staff and not lift a finger. The man who said this, one of our hosts, said we had all fought a hard fight against cancer and that we would now be treated— at which point he choked up and excused himself for crying and several of us had wet eyes too. I am doing the same as I write this. (I always blame the tears on my Irish heritage!)

We were told about the entire gourmet meal by the chef before he and his wife served it. It was a masterpiece involving a garlic sauced chicken thigh and many other culinary delights. I had a memorable orange chocolate tart for dessert!

After dinner we were treated to exceptional, unique and very, memorable entertainment provided by four musicians who played authentic Irish tunes in front of that cheery fireplace. It was truly beautiful and ranged from a mournful chant (a capella!) to an Irish polka, if you can believe it. We were told that Irish music is for dancing, so Mark started doing the polka with us.

I asked if they could play, "The Irish Washer Woman" because my cute little Mother with her beautiful, shapely legs, used to come in the room in her high heels and frilly little apron which she would lift with both hands and do this dance alternating legs with pointed toes--now in front, now behind—while singing a melody. They asked me to sing it and once I did they remembered it and played it twice through. It was wonderful for me!

After the entertainment we filed outside and up the steep hill to our cars for the short drive to our cabins. These small wooden structures consisted of 300 to 400 square feet and were a tribute to man's ingenuity in fitting the bare necessities of life into a walk-in closet sized space! The living room consisted of a hanging thumping gas stove, futon, BASIC kitchen, and one small chair. There were 2 bedrooms about 8'x9', one with double bed, dresser and nothing else but a midget closet, and the other room even smaller had 2 bunk beds. The bathroom was indescribably minute with a sink just big enough to spit in, a commode jutting out from the corner and almost into the tiny (you couldn't turn around in it really!) shower. How we three women managed is nothing short of a miracle.

My cabin mates, Tina and Waltina, had worked

together for a company that owns Massanutten Resort, so they knew each other well. Tina was a very petite little gal so she fit in the space better than we did. She was a coffee addict so that was the first thing on her list to fix every morning! Waltina was an African American who was an evangelistic preacher. She would say funny things. She called me "Baby" and seemed liked a caring, motherly type. She couldn't believe she was living with no television.

Tina had one eye which appeared to be crossed and she later told us that her husband was blind. Neither of them had traveled much. We were such different people, but we had all been through the same dire illness and it seemed to blend us into a much more homogenous unit than we would have been otherwise. Interesting.

We had a rough night adjusting to a strange bed, rain on the roof, the bumpty-banging of the gas stove, and occasional creaking sounds that no one understood but were peculiar to Cabin 4.

The next morning after wrestling into and out of the closet-bathroom and gulping Tina's black coffee into which several grounds had drifted, we drove to the lodge for (wait for it!) a gourmet breakfast! The food committee wouldn't let up. I couldn't resist the sausage casseroles, mini pancakes, and all the wonderful treats.

We then divided into two groups of six each for the fly-fishing adventure. I drew the fly- tying lesson in the lodge for my first event along with five others and the remainder of our group left for the river bank for lessons in casting a line and learning to fly fish. In the afternoon we would change places.

The world's calmest, most patient and soft-spoken man taught us to tie flies. Not one of us had ever done it, which was good. We were seated at a rectangular table, each with a vise in front of us. Squeezed in the vise was a barbed hook. Standing behind each of us in turn, our teacher taught us the intricacies of tying tiny threads in clockwise and then counter-clockwise directions and then adding a shiny piece of chenille on top that would sparkle and attract the fish. Many of us had to start again after the whole thing would slip apart. In the end, we each accomplished this delicate task and to show for at least 20 minutes of concerted effort we had an inch long black threaded mess with a very sharp barbed hook at the end that we proudly displayed (while trying not to get hooked) on our fishing caps!

Through the heavy wooden door came two ladies carrying folded chairs, towels and other equipment which they proceeded to set up so we could have chair massages. What wonderful treats we were given!

Now it was time for another fabulous gourmet meal but this time prepared by "alumnae" of the program we were enjoying so much. When they asked what they could do to pay back the Martha Jefferson Hospital it was suggested that they furnish a luncheon meal and did they ever! About eight ladies appeared with beautiful home-made culinary masterpieces from fancy salads to delicious desserts. But what I'll never forget was the utter joy on their faces! Their whole bodies were smiling! They told us how much they absolutely loved doing it! Each had brought something that was one of their favorite recipes and we were overwhelmed! This time we went through a buffet line and were joined by those back from the river.

Now it was my turn to try fishing! I climbed into "Chubby's" truck and found him a most interesting guide. We chatted all the way to the riverbank and I found that he worked for People Places. Before doing such worthy work he had been a hard driving contractor building condos and other commercial real estate without resting—always pushing himself. Now he was relaxed and giving of himself and very happy.

When we reached the riverbank, he parked under

a leafy branch, grabbed the rods and we crossed the country road to the riverbank. With such ease he cast his line far out into the current and taught me my first lesson. All my life I had imagined that one put the rod up high over the shoulder and heaved the line with mighty strength. Nothing could have been further from the truth! Using the elbow as a pivot, one slings the line sideways, picking a spot way out where one hopes the fly will land. This really takes practice! I also observed that he and the other guide in our group wouldn't stop at that. Once the fly was in a good spot, they wiggled the line slightly in an effort to imitate a real fly's movements. Chubby said that fish are smart and if you left your fly sitting and it made a letter "V" in the water, no fish would be fooled into thinking it was a real fly because they don't make v's in the water. I knew that fish were curious but would never have labeled them "smart." So much to learn!

Chubby and I both saw my fly bob, but I wasn't quick enough so my catch got away!

It seemed like an eternity until I got my next nibble and fortunately Chubby deftly yanked my line and said, "Now reel it in!"

Believe it or not, I did, and it was a gorgeous, iridescent rainbow trout with sun on every colorful scale. I know he was at least a foot long!  Really!

Shortly after that it was time to go so I clambered back into the truck, without my trophy because it was a "catch and release" stream.

Every one of us was laughing and recounting our individual fish tales when we gathered back at the main lodge.

Then we drove back to our cabins to clean up for dinner. That sounds easy, but it was nothing of the kind with three women of various shapes and sizes and a bathroom of one size—minute. I'm willing to bet it was no bigger than 4X6. Hall closets are larger!

Finally we were ready so we joined others on the comfortable porch of the lodge above the sparking lake waters. A kayak glided by, the perfect grace note.

We sipped wine and soft drinks and found that somehow, effortlessly and mysteriously, we had bonded. We were all perfectly comfortable with each other. I could have sat at any of the tables and enjoyed everyone seated there.

After another beautiful meal together, we enjoyed the program given by a fearless couple who trained falcons. These fierce looking birds perched on their gloves. We learned many interesting facts about them but were a little skittish to be seated so near them. Their handlers wanted us to put on their gloves and let the large black birds sit on them but we were hesitant. Suddenly it hit me that this whole weekend was about bravery so I stepped forward. I admit that I felt nervous at first, but the bird and I finally bonded to some degree—not as much as I did with dogs and, to a lesser degree, cats. I'm glad that I didn't wimp out, at least!

Saying good-bye to my cabin mates was a little harder than I'd thought after just three days with them, but the experience was unifying and I felt I'd known them much longer and indeed, I'd learned so much about them in that short time!  I had absolutely nothing in common with them except for a very important thing—surviving a dread disease. Nothing could have bound us tighter!

# Life With Father

It's hard to pick one adjective to describe Dad for he was a man of many talents and interests. I guess I would select "creative" to encompass an all over look at his skill set.

As I look back, I realize what a complex man Dad really was and as an adult I can analyze him so much more clearly than I could as a child and as a teenager. With understanding comes forgiveness, and that's a good thing!

It would take an immense array of adjectives to describe him, while Agatha Christie used one to describe her father: "agreeable." She loved that word and its application to him.

I would have a whole paragraph bursting with adjectives and still not quite have an adequate supply! Here are a few that come quickly to mind: talented, artistic, creative, etymologist, hardworking, proud, athletic, poetic, supercilious, persevering, determined, aesthetic, naive, superior, manic-depressive (or bi-polar, as it's now labeled) and frustrated.

I believe that his first disappointment was finding

out that although he was considered a very talented artist at home (he had won a scholarship for his talent to the Colorado School of Mines), he went off to New York's Art Students League thinking he would bowl them over there too, but he realized that there were many, many others there who were equally talented.

He came home to Omaha after that and was able to work as a commercial artist in the advertising business which was satisfying for him.

Then when I came along, the income wasn't sufficient so fortunately he was able to climb the ladder there and create ads plus get into management.

The next trauma occurred after we moved to Indianapolis, when my father decided that so many clients were asking for him that he needed to start his own ad agency. My mother was terribly upset by this because it was a very competitive business and such a huge gamble when he had the two of us to educate. That was the only time I ever heard them fight and they had a real brouhaha! They had closed the kitchen doors and I was doing homework in the living room, and could hear every word. I was so upset!

My dad ended up renting a space for his business over The Traction Terminal Building way downtown that had big buses underneath. He had several secretaries and worked very hard, but there just wasn't enough business so he asked his old business bosses, The Bozell and Jacobs founders, if he could rejoin and they were happy to get him back.

Every now and then he would take us all for rides—Sunday rides in which we often walked through houses under construction. Floor plans absolutely fascinated both of my parents.

Once when he thought I had been surrounded by too much wealth he would drive us to a very poor, blighted neighborhood so we could see how lucky we were.

They enjoyed open houses so much that they became "regulars" in the eyes of some of the realtors who knew that they weren't going to buy a house but rather they became friends and enjoyed seeing each other.

One particular Sunday Mother's cousin Michael and his wife, Pat, asked if they would like to go with them as they were really house hunting and Mother and Dad eagerly responded in the affirmative. When they descended on the third house for the day, Mother and Dad kept punching each other as they would see features that they loved. As they were getting ready to depart, they asked Pat and Mike how they liked the house and the answer came back, "Oh, this isn't at all what we're looking for." Mother and Dad whooped,

"Good! Because we want to buy it!" They just loved it as it had a step down living room with stained glass window designs in the upper portion, a lovely long patio with a charming backyard, and many other features they liked. It was on a wonderful street that got almost no traffic, between two wider thoroughfares and Mother called it, "Dear Little Delaware." It was a very happy move for them as they had many neighbors who became good friends.

Meanwhile, Michael and Pat decided to build the perfect house for them and their three teenage daughters that had an entirely different floor plan on three large levels, so everyone was happy!

Oh, and I'm sure that many realtors were buzzing about the Gallups' finally buying a house, after going to open houses for about 20 years.

One day Dad came bursting into the house with even more enthusiasm than usual!

"Jane" he cried. "Guess what? This year the garden tour will be featuring the Meridian-Kessler neighborhood! I really think we should be on it, don't you?"

My mother, who would describe herself as the opposite of creative and certainly no gardener, often said she was a "house plant." She actually never ventured into the yard and would have flunked a question about what a trowel was. She kept the neatest house in town and visions of muddy-footed strangers trooping over the Orientals held little charm for her. Besides, she would be very occupied with the World Series during that time frame. She must have swallowed hard but she said, "How nice" or something equally pleasing.

The great day arrived and thankfully, the weather was fine—bright blue October weather. The guide led the first visitors through the living room.

"Oh" said one of the ladies. "How nice—what a lovely grand piano. Does Mrs. Gallup play?"

The guide said, "No Mr. Gallup plays the piano."

They went into the dining room next.

"What a lovely painting," continued the guest. "Is Mrs. Gallup an artist?"

"No," said the guide, "Mr. Gallup paints portraits and still lifes."

Opening the French doors to the patio, the visitors had an enchanted view of the garden. "My, my, they murmured, Mrs. Gallup has made a lovely garden!"

At this point the guide laughed and said, "Mr. Gallup is the gardener. That's Mrs. Gallup in the den yelling her head off watching the World Series."

When Dad turned 50 he bought a car and what a story that was! He left the house one day, telling

Mother that it was time for him to trade cars and that he was going to get another Buick. Off he went, and he was so surprised to see a cute little convertible in the window next to a Buick sedan. He asked the salesman what kind it was and was told it was a Fiat.

Dad said, "It's really cute! I bet it's terribly expensive!"

The salesman, who really "saw him coming" said, "No actually it's the same price as that Buick sedan."

Dad started salivating and said he would just like to sit in it. He started playing with the buttons and was fascinated by the ashtray that came out clean after it had ashes in it and you pushed it forward. He laughed and said, "Little Italians sweep it out." He was enchanted and said that he was going to buy it on the spot instead of that stodgy old sedan. On the way home, he stopped and bought a funny hat with big eyes in front that moved around. Mother couldn't believe her eyes when he came tooting down the driveway!

After that he wanted to drive it everywhere so Mother had to buy a scarf (she hated scarves) because he wanted her to accompany him on some sales trips.

Not long after this, Mother noticed that Dad seemed to be undergoing some serious changes. He had always been a live wire and loved to entertain and play the piano, but he started staying out very late and sleeping just a few hours at night, but the worst of it was that he started bringing in lots of people while she was trying to sleep. Suddenly the house would be full of complete strangers all singing around the piano at 2 AM. Mother was really frightened and didn't know what to do.

He did other strange things, too, like buying her very expensive jewelry and evening dresses. I remember a long black velvet "hostess gown" with a gold belt that she would never have wanted to slink around in. She didn't want to hurt his feelings, but she certainly didn't want the very expensive and inappropriate gifts—plus they had a joint checking account and she had no idea what he was spending—she was the bookkeeper and he was the spendthrift.

Suddenly this wild behavior was replaced by sadness and depression and Dad would sit in the den playing moody records by Frank Sinatra and drink cream sherry, of all things. All the green leather couch cushions got sticky from where he spilled it. During this time, he didn't want to go anywhere or talk to anyone.

If this sounds like bi-polar, or as it was known in those days, manic-depressive behavior, it was. Mother was beginning to suspect that, but in any case, she knew he was very, very sick and she needed to get him to a psychiatrist. It's one thing to know it and quite another to get him to a doctor. Neither of my parents EVER went to a doctor (Mother always said "he might find something"), so now she had to figure out how to pull this off. The plan was to convince Dad that all the employees at the ad agency were going to need to get physicals for insurance purposes and then, somehow, get him into a psychiatrist's office from there.

It all fell into place and suddenly Dad was in LaRue Carter, a mental hospital. His doctor there explained to Mother that this manic-depressive illness really only occurs with very intelligent creative people who just cross that line and get sick. At that time they had just come out with lithium which was a powerful drug that had to be carefully monitored so as to have just the right amount for each individual.

It had a very bad side effect because while making the "highs" lower and the "lowness" higher to try to even it out – the result robbed a person of those creative genius moments which were so necessary to get exciting ideas that Dad used in the ads he created. He said, "The ideas just won't come any more."

Sadly, he had to stay in that hospital for months and not only did he hate it and became very sad while there, but he had to miss my sister's wedding which was a terrible blow.

I went to see him when I was visiting in Indiana to relieve Mother from going every day. It was such a hard thing to do, but of course I was happy to relieve Mother at least a little bit.

Mother was a little uptight about the flowers and the yard since my sister's wedding reception was at the house so fortunately the groom's father stepped in and helped with those details. I was the Matron of Honor and very early in my pregnancy so I was as happy as could be and we all rallied around and made the best of things.

When Dad was released from the hospital he had follow-up appointments with the doctor who kept a close check on the lithium level. He did seem more like himself, but he still couldn't pop out ideas so eventually the firm brought in a new creative director and started easing Dad out. This was very sad and it meant losing his 401K. Back in those days I don't think people had any recourse.

Well, to show you what my father was made of, he started to work again—this time selling IDS (Investor' Diversified Services) and learning all about selling stock plans. He also started a landscape consultant business and some other ventures. All this wasn't easy at his age by then, but he was determined. The last job

I remember his doing was working to secure housing for Indiana University students.

I didn't ever know that he had once taught advertising and public relations at Butler University during some evenings until someone told me.

My parents both smoked and in the end that was what got them. Both had emphysema, which is a terrible disease.

In their later years my parents moved to a one-story house with central air which they needed. My father fell in love with the backyard and the handsome brick patio and the fact that it had two dens so they could have one overlooking the patio, with TV where they could watch the evening news and enjoy cocktails, and the other with a piano and permanent card table which was called "the game room." Mother got a beautiful dining room banquet table with an inlay border for the dining room and although it had just two bedrooms, they were content. Once again they were on a shady, curving street behind the main street (North Meridian) so it was peaceful yet very convenient.

I was really shocked to hear about the real estate firm's approach to selling the "Dear Little Delaware" house. Mother said that the firm's realtors walked through and they all wrote down a sales figure on pieces of paper, threw the estimates of the sales price on the floor, then averaged them, and that's how they arrived at an asking price. I just cannot image anything worse. They put their faith in an old friend and former neighbor who was a realtor. My parents were such lovely, trusting people!

The home they chose had many excellent features for them in their old age, but it had one fairly large flaw, i.e. the laundry was in the basement, as was the case in older, charming homes. Also, my father wanted to continue painting portraits and still lifes, and there was no space except in the basement for his messy oils. One day he fell headlong down those steps and his voice floated up saying, "I'm fine—nothing is broken."

Mother loved to do any handwork like needlepoint and knitting and made my sister, my cousins, and me beautiful sweaters, afghans, and dressing stools. She also delighted in making Christmas stockings and hats for her granddaughters.

How cruel a hand was she dealt, then, when suddenly she couldn't see those stitches. Her first thought was that she needed new glasses, but after a trip to the ophthalmologist she was told that she had macular degeneration. I feel sure that it was caused by smoking. Dying by inches instead of all at once is a terrible fate!

She gave me an unfinished needlepoint project that I assured her I would do, but I never did, sadly.

She loved her bridge club so they bought cards with large print so she could keep playing. When she drove to bridge club she made all right turns and carefully planned her route that way as she couldn't see far enough to cross the street when turning left. Once she said to me, "Oh, those bikers! And those joggers! If they knew how poorly I can see they wouldn't be out there!"

Before we realized how bad her eyesight was, my sister and I were in the car with her and she kept changing lanes. My sister said, "Mother, you simply must choose one lane and keep in it."

Subsequently, a neighbor came outside and Mother told me that she wasn't sure if it was the wife or the husband and laughingly said, 'That's pretty bad."

In the end, this ophthalmologist wasn't able to do anything to help the problem and said that she would always see large objects and not fall over them.

Finally, she couldn't participate in driving to bridge nor seeing well enough to play and her friends told her that they would miss her pretty blue eyes. Mother kept her sadness to herself, but I know she cried!

Mother was a wonderful record keeper and would have made a superb accountant. She could do a lot of math in her head and she knew everyone's birthday and anniversary without one slip-up. She reminded me to turn the clock up or back each year when it was time. But the really amazing feat she performed was keeping the balances of checkbooks and savings books in her head when her vision started to be severely affected.

Once when I was visiting she said, "Honey, I hate to bother you with this because I know you hate math, but I think your father made a mistake in this checkbook." She remembered the balance and his subtraction to the penny and she was exactly right, of course.

Mother had a terrible occurrence that was a stroke while she was sitting in the bathtub. My father's approach to the situation was to wait until morning and see if she was better. Of course, this was the wrong thing to do as with passing time the effects became worse. They finally got to the hospital and my sister and I both rushed to Indianapolis. Mother brightened up considerably and told the nurses that her girls were coming!

The part of her brain that was affected by this sad occurrence was her speech and her condition was called "aphasia." Mother and I both loved word games so I was more able than most people to figure out how to work with it. (She also lost some of her memory, tragically).

I asked her if it was like seeing a noun clearly but being unable to say that word and she agreed enthusiastically and so we figured out how to give clues to the word. For instance, if she wanted to say June she could say "1,2,3,4,5,6 in the year" and, whereas Dad was in the dark, I could figure it out. She had a speech pathologist and many lessons but couldn't get back 100%.

This was a source of great frustration for her as was her inability to recall names that she knew so well. She would hit her head with her fist and say "dumb girl!" It would break your heart!

She was equally knowledgeable about the stock market and enjoyed Wall Street Week so much when it came on the air. She listened to both broadcasts after her stroke, trying so hard to completely process it.

Finally, the move had to take place for Mother to be in the nursing home so they did a lot of research before choosing one. Dad went to see her every single day and they shared many meals there. Mother would receive treatments on her chest to help her breathe. Emphysema kills you by inches.

I worried so about her in that nursing home, unable to read any more (which she loved) and with some memory loss.

She was tired of lobster and other delicacies served

there and yearned for old-fashioned pot roast!

Because her sense of hearing was still strong, I asked a friend how I could get a barbershop quartet to sing to her on her birthday. I was so glad that I pulled that one off.

After the hospital stay she was moved to a place where she had to do physical therapy that was a joke! This was apparently an insurance requirement. Mother hated physical exercise of any kind so she sort of fluffed her way through her lifting exercise as I noticed, going by in the hall. My father couldn't face the reality that she was not coming back home but would rather need nursing home care. I believe that there was a short period of time when she was trying to be at home but she had difficulties that were hard to address there. Her pillows had to get higher and higher, so she could breathe in bed with her emphysema.

They asked a young nurse if she could help them part time and she was glad to. They were quite pleased with her, but she began stealing money and other things. I made a quick trip home and grabbed jewelry and furs and fired the nurse and tried to get them meals on wheels. Dad shot that down declaring that it was charity and that he would NOT take charity. No amount of convincing on my part would dissuade him. They were both so frail at that point that they would split a chicken breast!

Mother's funeral was packed!!    I was distraught because she had told me that she wanted Ernest Lynch to be the minister if he was available. I turned over heaven and earth but couldn't locate him so we had a woman who hadn't known her. It nearly killed me. Someone in the funeral home had put orange lipstick on her that upset my daughter no end. She knew how "Gainey" hated the color orange!

My sister, father and I furnished the minister with a lot of details about mother's life and I brought up her presidency of The Orphan's Auxiliary and Dad said, "Oh, I'd forgotten that."

All I could think was, Yeah, you were so self-involved with all of your triumphs in the advertising world you didn't see Mother in the den, practicing her remarks with great fear and trembling at the thought of speaking in front of people!  No, it was all about him.

Dad must have been just terribly miserable alone in that house!  I can only imagine—and with no audience to play to!  He tried to continue his art studio experience, meaning that he loaded his canvas and oil paints into the car trunk and headed several miles up the road to a communal artists' mecca. There he would mingle with other artists and aspiring artists, and paint happily. They had models, which he enjoyed. I am sure he was regaling everyone with his anecdotes. He simply could not exist without human interaction, and (wait for it!) PRAISE!

One day he called me and said that he had picked out a retirement community and made a deposit on an apartment. Fortunately, I had prepared well in advance of this day by going to the Indianapolis Board of Realtors, showed them my credentials, and sitting in their spacious office building looking up realtors. After about 17 years in the business at that point I knew exactly what qualities in a realtor I was looking for and I had preselected one!  Just one out of thousands!  I needed the right professional degrees, the right number of years in the business, and someone who really knew how desirable that location was in a city so huge— someone from that neighborhood. I was lucky to find anyone who met my rigorous standards!

And was I right!  She examined the appraisal and increased the asking price by about $10,000 due to its location and demand for it. She felt it in her bones because she grew up there. (Now you can see why "Willow" has no real value for pricing neighborhoods all over the country!  What a joke!)

I was so happy that Dad really liked the lady I had

chosen to handle the sale of his beloved home and he cheerfully signed the paperwork and made his formal application at the retirement location. The showing went well and in a fairly short time he received a good offer from a lawyer and signed it. Meanwhile, he made frequent trips to his chosen destination and then, out of the blue one day, he called me long distance and told me that he had changed his mind and decided to stay in his house and not sell.

My first thought was of Mother and how she would have rolled her eyes—she was so much more astute with business!  She would have chimed in, "Just like your Father!"  My second thought was, How could this happen to ME, a realtor!  I said, "Dad, what made you change your mind?"

He answered that he had decided too quickly. That was all, and that he was sure the Buyer "would understand!"

Oh, yeah, I thought – the buyer who happened to be a lawyer!

I said, "Dad, I will ask the realtor there to visit with you and go over things and I'll come and visit, too." I panicked big time and called Dad's realtor. We decided that we would both sit down with him the next evening. We were so worried!

Sure enough after I drove to Indy the next day, we sat down in the game room at a card table with his contract of sale staring up at us!

Slowly we stepped him through it and explained that it was a binding document. At last he agreed to go ahead with his move and I assured him that both of his daughters would help.

My sister was very helpful and had marvelous organizational skills. We had to let a lady who did estate sales handle much of it and away went furniture and other items that neither my sister or I had room for. It was so sad saying goodbye to paintings and objects of art from our childhood and the books! Oh, the books! We had to give many away for a song. They marched up the entire length of the front walk. That killed us more than anything.

# II.

# Real Estate

Some psychological observations from my thirty-six years of practice.

I cannot tell you how many military officers and CEO's—people used to being in charge—have been very problematic in the sale of their principal residences. They simply aren't used to allowing anyone else to take complete charge; therefore, the best tactic for a realtor is to schedule a long meeting with this seller, making suggestions and tossing them the ball so that they will feel that it's their idea!

NEVER go in swinging and telling this seller that you're an expert in this field (even though you should be and probably are).

It is also wise to invite this seller's cooperation in making a list of printed information regarding the home's features to give the prospective buyers. Some sellers like to list improvements they have made to the property and include the dates for each.

They may also list factual information about their location such as distance to schools, shopping, interstates, etc.

Other ideas for sellers who really want control might be (and I have seen all of these):

a diagram and names of all the plantings in the yard, a personalized note about some of the things they have enjoyed about living here such as the sunsets from the patio, a list of repairmen who have installed roofing, appliances, etc. It is also helpful to have a kitchen drawer with the garage door opener, extra keys, warranties and instruction books for appliances.

The best advice is, of course, to leave for the showings!! You can explain that if the buyer wants to see all the wonderful features of the home if the floor plan works for him so in that case he will want to open all the closets and kitchen cabinets. If the seller is there, even in a different room, he will feel intrusive, invasive and downright rude doing so and he will never buy unless he does that! He may even want to sit in a comfortable chair in the family room and just look out or around. (This is a very good buying sign). He would not want to do that if you're there. Most sellers get this once you cheerfully explain that.

Once I showed a house to a couple and the wife made very small little guttural noises like "Um hum" as she glided through the rooms. I later learned that the husband didn't want her to say anything because she had exclaimed enthusiastically about a house they bought the last time and he thought they paid too much because the sellers had been in earshot and knew how much she liked it.

I encouraged husbands who were looking at houses prior to the wife's trip to see them to make an offer subject to her approval in a certain time period because that was a legal contingency which would hold the house for them if the seller agreed to the price and terms. This worked like a charm 99% of the time, but one time the transferring gentleman loved the house (and the garage, of course!) so he wrote an offer subject to his wife's approval. When I took her through it later she shook her head in the small, narrow kitchen and exclaimed, "I wonder why in this green earth he thought I would like this house!"

It just proves that there is truly an exception to every rule, even when you think you know each other after having lived together for 18 years!

# What Are the Pilot's Duties?

Now let me ask you what duties the pilot of your plane has? Does he make your reservation, print your boarding pass, load your luggage onto the plane, serve snacks and drinks, etc. or does he simply fly the plane?

Yet this is what people expect of a realtor and sometimes we fall into this trap and end up writing ads at midnight because there simply was no time during the action-packed day.

When computers came on the scene it became obvious that we couldn't spend our time out pressing the flesh and looking for leads in the computer and carry them both off really well.

There are many auxiliary positions that can be filled by the right person that will free up the realtor to mix and mingle, join organizations, and list & sell property.

It would be an over simplification if I left it at that. You can hire people to fill slots such as buyer specialist(s), transaction specialist, runner, executive assistant, etc. but unless they are family members who know how you work and what you expect, it's difficult to get people who share your vision and your work ethic!  I had three or four executive assistants before I got the right one as well as several buyer specialists.

You must spend your time on activities that result in earning money since there is no salary. Writing ads and putting signs in the ground do not earn you money. I realize that this sort of thing must be delegated— particularly putting signs in, taking them out, hanging key safes on doors, and all that—so I hired a gal who knew the county quite well to take ads to the paper and all the tasks that required running around.

My executive assistant saved me from burial alive! I had tried several who were not satisfactory, but the third was the charm and we stayed together for about 18 years!  She had been executive secretary to nine vice presidents at once in a corporate setting, so she was terribly underemployed with me!

She was so good that she had a tray on the desk with paper work for long range projects and she would reach into that when all the immediate tasks were completed. (Her idea).

She freed me up to get new business while she politely called our sellers to give them feedback on showings of their property. Sometimes she had to call the realtor who showed our listing repeatedly to get what his buyer's comments were, too!

My sellers enjoyed her calls; she was so personable on the phone.

She reminded me of all kinds of things like deadlines and was absolutely invaluable!

Real estate around here peaked in value—the demand became greater than the supply—in 2005 and 2006 ,which changed the playing field as well as the rules! Competition for property became fierce.

Some realtors didn't adjust to the change and kept writing the same verbiage in their contracts, which did not serve their buyers well!

Now it was necessary to use an acceleration clause—clean from the big cities in Northern Virginia—which addressed the fact that there might be competing offers submitted at the same time and if so, how high the bidder was willing to go and in what increments, whether he would eliminate a home inspection, etc. It was wild for our little town.

One day my assistant hit upon a very useful discovery and I don't know that anyone else did! She said, "I've found that if I go into the Multiple Listing site about 4:00 I can see what's getting ready to come out tomorrow!"

Wow! This was fantastic news!

For example, I had three clients looking for historic

homes in the downtown area—scarce as the proverbial hens' teeth—and my assistant found several this way on different days. I raced to the phone and called my buyer clients and advised them to drop everything and go with me that evening and to write an offer immediately if they liked it because the next day everyone would know about it and they would be in competition and could lose it. My clients were eternally grateful to me for this service and I so grateful to my assistant!

Now it should be dawning on the realtor that part time realtors are doing a terrible disservice to their clients. This has never been and will never be "something to do in my spare time." Realtors are supposed to be agents for their clients, which they can't possibly be if they're not on top of the market as well as being well informed about the industry with its constant changes.

# How Do You Choose Your Doctor?

Was it because he or she sits next to you in church or is your son's Cub Scout Leader? I ask because these are some of the answers I get when I ask how a person chose their realtor to sell their house. It illustrates clearly that we're comfortable choosing someone "like me." Realtors have fought this concept for many years with ads about their professional designations and their meaning. It seems to fall on deaf ears for the most part, but I submit that for many people their home represents their largest, most important investment, and to entrust its care to just anyone with a real estate license can be one of your most costly mistakes!

So, what's important to look for when you make your selection? When I needed laparoscopic surgery for a painful gall stone I went to a surgeon whom I knew personally as well as by reputation and I asked him point blank how many of these surgeries he had performed and if they were all successful. He answered, "That's fair." And he had done many hundreds.

Experience is very important when you choose an

agent to represent you in real estate, but it's not the only factor by any means. You should see what professional designations the realtor holds for several reasons.

- This person has invested considerable time and money to acquire this knowledge, knowledge that can protect you in this very important transaction.
- This person can see red flags while they're still yellow and head off possible problems and he or she can make sure that the wording in your listing and sales contracts is understood by you and is protective of your best interests.

You should also look for leadership roles in organizations the realtor belongs too, which show an interest in his or her community.

As in the practice of law, realtors' interests and fields of expertise vary widely. I know men for example, who hate to show land and get "their trouser cuffs dirty" and I wouldn't want to list my county acreage with them. (Conversely, I know a man who was a very successful realtor who loved only land and called me if it had a house on it to list the house).

There are realtors who specialize in historic homes and those who really prefer brand new ones. And of course, the commercial realtor is another breed of cat!

As a referral realtor I can access all of this information quite easily and it's free to the client.

# Making Marriages in My Dishpan

I have found that when I do dishes, it frees up my mind to wander and do some serious problem-solving.

On this particular day, I'd had some old friends come to me with a specific buying request but with a strict budget. At first glance, it seemed like an insolvable problem.

They had beautiful antiques and knew that the heat system must be radiator hot water because hot air would dry them out. They needed several fairly large rooms to display their Oriental rugs. But the real kicker was that they needed to be not too far from horseback riding which was their passion!

At first blush this was an impossible combination because when horses entered the picture, we most certainly would be in the county on some acreage, and land would drive the price even higher. I had shown them several possibilities, hoping to increase their budgetary restraints, but to no avail.

I started dwelling on the problem as I did dishes. Suddenly, a house with an adequately sized living and dining room and radiators with hot water heat floated into my mind. I knew it well since it was my listing. Alas! It was about $5,000 too high. I stewed over that and also remembered how firm the owners were on their price.

I decided to visit these homeowners and talk about the listing again. I remarked that they had included a washer, dryer, and other appliances and wondered aloud if they could keep them and offer their home for $5,000 less?

(The reason I really wanted this to work was that the home was in walking distance of a horse farm!)

The owners agreed to this new plan and both buyers and sellers were absolutely delighted!

My happiness was complete when my old real estate course teacher, who saw the sale go through, complimented me with a congratulatory phone call! "Nice sale," he said.

# A Memorable Shower

Some old and dear friends listed their beautiful 2 story traditional brick home with me and I was delighted to go to work for such great people.

One day the lady of the house was upstairs in the shower when she heard the loudest crash imaginable and thought,

"WHAT WAS THAT??"

What had happened really needs to be shown in slow motion movie—words cannot describe it—and the movie makers in Hollywood would have rejected this script as just too impossible! I will nevertheless attempt to describe it in my poor words.

Across the street was another house situated on a corner lot. The two driveways were across from each other.

In the house across the street lived a local car dealer, his wife, and their young son. Said young son came home and left his car in the driveway without putting the emergency brake on. Said car slowly began to roll backwards. It crossed the hump in the middle of the street and headed straight for the garage. This was a two-car garage in my friends' home with a brick post in the center, separating the two spaces. The car went in the opening on the right side perfectly, not even grazing the center post, and crashed through the fireplace into the living room which was under the master suite, and of course, the shower!

As a P.S., we had to stop all showings until a new garage wall and a new fireplace were built! The man of the house told me that was the strongest fireplace wall in the State of Virginia!

# Regarding Buyers

Typically, so many realtors go through their entire career not getting it. I have heard so many say, "All buyers are liars." This simply isn't the case at all.

All realtors need to listen to what buyers say they are looking for and then they need to keep asking questions. They need to understand the buyer's motivation. Is this a job promotion? Is this a downsize move for some reason? Is this buyer buying safety for his children in a dead-end street situation?

You see, buyers will always compromise specification but they will NEVER compromise motivation.

To illustrate:

A buyer moving here from out of state who is an officer in a large corporation says, "I must have a living room that's at least 15' X 20'. "

Your average realtor will go through listing after listing trying to find those measurements that's specified.

What's the motivation? Well, he's been given a new position and a raise so he wants to have an impressive home to entertain members of his company.

You sell the house you hope he'll buy like this:

Drive down the street saying, "Hi, Dr. Smith."

You can add, "He's such a nice fellow." Drive further and, if you don't see the people, explain who the neighbors are ("That's where Judge Brown lives."). By the time you reach the driveway, you have it sold.

I once had the assignment of finding a home for the incoming officer of a college and his wife, a music professor. They had a collection of 2,000 books that had to be housed and they only liked newer homes— oh, and it had to be about five minutes from the college. This was such a tall order because the homes near the college were historic and dated from about 1800 to 1920. They were architecturally amazing and highly desirable for most people but not for them! There was only one newer neighborhood that might work, but nothing there was for sale. They absolutely had to identify a home before leaving town to go back to their present college jobs so we earmarked one that was a little too far and a little too small. They left town putting on a brave smile.

Two days later the perfect home came on the market in that neighborhood where nothing had been for sale! I called and said, "Your house just came on the market! Can you come?"

They responded that they would love to, but they couldn't leave the college where they worked again so soon! They said, "Take pictures! Send them!"

I wasted no time. I took pictures of the surroundings as well as every room in the house including bathrooms and laundry.

They were overjoyed and decided they could have bookshelves built in the walk-out basement and did I know someone who could build them?

Yes, I did!

They said, "Mail the contract!"

(I did!)

They wanted a home inspection so when we coordinated that with their arrival date here (with their furniture in a truck!) I told them I'd meet them at the house with the inspector. So there they were, on the doorstep waiting to see their home for the first time!

I held my breath as we paraded through it and they said things like, "Oh, this must be a linen closet. Oh, these steps must go to an outside basement entrance."

Fortunately, they really liked it! Phew! What a responsibility!


Here's a true story that's hard to believe! One morning I got a phone call from somewhere in England and was pleased to hear that lovely British accent on the other end. This man declared enthusiastically: "We've just viewed our dream house on your web site!"

I could hardly wait to continue this conversation!

"Yes," he went on, "It's the lovely large white one with dark green shutters! It's perched on lush acreage above the road. It has an inviting patio in back and it's only two years old!"

"Well," I answered, "are you moving to the states?"

"Yes," he said, "my wife is from the Charlottesville area, which wouldn't be far, and that is exactly the type of home we want."

"Great," I continued. "But you're in England. How soon can you see it?"

He said, "I can be there in two days. I've been to Staunton before and I know where the train station is. I could meet you there."

Then he added, "I will carry a copy of The London Times under my arm that should make identification certain."

"Oh," I mused, "how marvelously British!"

It all seemed like a dream and I wondered if this would actually happen! With racing heart (and a key to the white house), I drove to the station at the appointed hour. I beheld a tall, stately gentleman in a business suit carrying a furled umbrella (of course!) with the

London Times under his other arm! Oh, sheer delight! We talked a lot about London (I had been there several times) and drove along the scenic road to this property about five miles west of town.

He was very happy to see it in person and carefully explored each room, explaining that since his wife couldn't come, he would have to phone her and describe the details.

Back to my office we went and made a long, long, long distance call. I tried not to think of dollar signs with wings on them!

Her reaction was very favorable so she told him to go ahead and buy it! I'll never forget that thrill!

I once had the pleasure of getting to know an elderly gentleman who had grown up in the Staunton area and told me interesting stories of the old days. One of these was regarding Lindbergh's visit. His father had gotten him out of school so he could meet the great man when he flew his famous plane to a long, grassy spot near Deerfield and landed. He was the guest of a prominent Staunton citizen who had a summer retreat there and Lindbergh would be able to relax, hunt and fish.

The elderly gentleman told me that he had served in the CIA and had had a most interesting career but had come back home to retire and also buy a home for his sister and her husband who had fallen on hard times— in fact, they had to soon be out of their home. He had cash to buy a nice place for them and was happy that he could do so.

He did specify that he wanted one particular lawyer—a woman—and no one else so he wrote a contract and when it was accepted I delivered it to his lawyer. We looked forward to a quick closing.

The home he had selected was a nice brick ranch west of town with a mountain view, some acreage that featured a tennis court near the road, and attractive landscaping.

It all seemed so simple!   That's when you have to watch out, I guess!   He had chosen this lawyer for a good reason:  She was very thorough. She worked way ahead of closing and was just one of those well-organized people.

Several weeks before the big day she let us know there was a title problem – a big one!  It seemed that the Highway Department had never officially closed off the old state highway that once ran through this property (right through the tennis courts!) so theoretically they could reopen it at any time. Now, we know that as a practical matter this "ain't happenin'"; however, it was a huge blemish on the title and every buyer wants a clear title and its assurance (an insurance!)

She told us that she would submit everything to VDOT (The Highway powers that be) in Richmond and that when they put it on the docket they would most likely clear it.

So, I wondered, how soon would this take place? It turned out not to be a matter of great urgency to them so we waited all summer long before those poor folks could move in!

"It Ain't Closed 'Til It's Closed!"

As a P.S. I can't resist telling you that the subject property had been sold twice in the past 10 years and male lawyers who searched the title for those two buyers did not find the cloud on the title!

(If you liked these stories, I wrote a separate book on real estate, How to Sell for More and Buy for Less, that has some of these stories and others!)

*faces*
OF HOPE

# III.

# Travel

# Is Bermuda still Paradise?

I first went out of the country in October of 1958 when my husband and I gaily sailed from Norfolk to Bermuda on the SS Arosa Sky. I looked critically at some of the bolts on deck and commented that they looked quite rusty. (Later I learned that this was that old tub's last voyage!)  I think it had played a role (probably very minor) in WWII. Undeterred, we met up with some other orthodontists and their wives in the lounge for a mambo lesson. At this moment the voyage became a bit rough as we were heading into fairly large waves. It became quite funny to start dancing in one spot and then suddenly be in a higher spot, still dancing.

At this point there was a contest announced in which volunteers did their own dances. I did my solo Charleston number in spite of the pitching of the boat and was rewarded with first prize: a bottle of champagne. It was amazing to see how many good friends I suddenly was blessed with!  Many chairs were pulled up to our table and glasses were poured until it was all gone, or should I say, "Down the hatch"?

After that we were invited to a friend's cabin for a

drink of whiskey and I learned that a blend of scotch and bourbon wasn't for me. I have never been able to swallow scotch!

We tottered off to our cabin and suddenly the ship began to pitch and roll violently. We were in a hurricane! I have never been more nauseated. Our rooms had no bathroom which added to our problems. The stewards placed buckets up and down the hallways for seasickness.

My husband said he was fine just as long as he remained prone on his bunk, but if he even sat up, he was sick. I was sick in any position! The next morning I decided that fresh air would help so I staggered down the narrow hallway, bouncing from side to side and trying not to bump the buckets, until I reached the steep, narrow stairway at the end which led to the deck in the bow. I lurched up the stairway and out onto the deck. Grasping the railing on the port side I turned and looked up at the Captain high above me. Guess what? HE was sick also! Now, that was a bad hurricane! The fresh air really didn't help so I fell back into my bunk.

Eventually we came out of it and docked peacefully in Hamilton. All was forgotten as we absorbed the fairyland beauty of the harbor and surrounding pastel colored houses – pink, green, powder blue, yellow, turquoise! And each one had a sparkling white molded roof – looking like plaster—with gutters to catch the fresh water that was very precious there. That was the only way to get it!

The glistening blue water was picture perfect, but beyond it lay pink sand which was a breathtaking sight and then to gaze out at the waters of the ocean was an unbelievable picture! Near the pink beach the water was a light turquoise and as you looked further away the shade deepened slowly until it became a rich royal blue far out. I had never seen these gorgeous colors before! I could have stayed longer, but it was time to explore this paradise!

All of our friends were renting mopeds so we did too although we had never ridden one before so we took a quick lesson. We had to learn quickly and well because many of the narrow roads had a high stone or coral wall along the side that would have been terrible to hit. We paid attention because there had been fatalities. To add to the challenge, there were traffic circles (called "round-abouts") and, since the island was English, one had to drive on the left side of the road and negotiate the circles backwards (or so it seemed to us). Finally we ventured forth for a beautiful ride to admire the sparkling sea and pastel houses and eventually we arrived at one of the recommended sites: the perfume factory. This wasn't at all like it sounded but was mainly a showroom featuring perfume made from island flowers. That was the strongest, most over powering perfume aroma I had ever been acquainted with! If, it had been a noise instead of a scent, it would have been deafening!  In spite of this, I bought a small souvenir bottle.

Back in the storybook town of Hamilton we parked our mopeds and dropped into the Hog Penny Pub. (I loved the name!)  We had a good lunch and then took in some great shopping. It was time for another education about that!  Being an island, so many things were imported which makes them for expensive in a retail setting; however, if they came from the British Isles, they weren't terribly expensive. Woolens of all kinds were not terribly pricey nor was Scotch (ugh), but a lot of the food products had to be imported so dining was costly. They also had an interesting rule instituted by cab drivers: it was one fare before midnight but much higher after the bewitching hour. And speaking of cabs, they were adorable!  They all looked like the surrey with the fringe on top and were so colorful— each one a different hue!

That first evening we went to the Carlton Beach

Hotel where we sat outside at a romantic table for two lit by a candle afloat in a vase of water and we ordered one of those heavenly rum drinks that they fix so well in the "islands" with all kinds of fresh fruit juices. It was called the "Love Potion" and came in a huge hollowed out coconut shell with two straws!

Just then the Talbot Brothers came onto a small stage and serenaded us with songs that were typical of Bermuda—they had a very mellow blend of voices. I loved "Bermuda Buggy Ride" and "Yellow Bird" and "Man, Man is for the Woman Made" and "Man Smart—Woman Smarter!" and "Mama Don't Want No Peas, No Rice." I can still remember their beauty, drifting over the warm breezes.

The next night we were treated to the Esso Steel Drums—actual steel drums. The islanders played with marked off notes on the top. They could play everything from "Malaguena" to "Yellow Bird" with their cloth-wrapped drumsticks hitting the right notes on the drum top. It is such a treat and pure magic to witness their talent!

At night you could hear the tree frogs croaking rhythmically and smell the perfumed flowers: in the daytime the hibiscus with its bright pink blooms, the clusters of bananas up high in the trees, the sail boats dancing in the breeze, all wove a spell that would stay with us.

We told our friends from Richmond about it when we got home. We talked them right into going with us several years later instead of going to Virginia Beach at the same time. We sang praises of the Bermuda paradise so they agreed to go! Their daughter was 10 and our daughter, Debbie, was three. Our party also included my mother-in-law who would delight in helping to look after Debbie. As luck would have it, once again we arrived in a hurricane, but this time we were flying. We had to circle for a while and then dart down for a landing. The rain was coming down in sheets, so we hurried to the Edgewater Beach Hotel. I was so disappointed for our friends, not being able to see the island from the air!

We arrived in the hotel lobby, rather tired and very wet, and asked about our room. We were to have stayed in one of the garden apartments down on the beach, but the people hadn't checked out yet so they wanted to put us up in the main hotel. The desk clerk was very courteous and apologetic and had a lovely English accent. My husband was furious and appealed to his friend from Richmond, a realtor, to do something, but he said there wasn't anything to do about it.

At last we went upstairs to our quarters and I was

just glad to get into dry clothes.

We had a lovely dinner, as always in Bermuda. It was a training ground for waiters who came from many different countries and that was interesting, too. They were always young and handsome.

The next day we went for a dip in the pool that, like the hotel, was on a high point on the island with a commanding view of the pink sand beach and aqua waters. It was a salt-water pool since water is so precious there and I found it difficult for swimming.

At last our garden apartments were ready so we unpacked everything and got settled. We had lunch at an informal place by the water and met up with the English sparrows for the first time. If you dined outside they would swoop down on your food so you were always shooing them off! I guess it was before credit cards because our friend leaned over and $1,000 slipped out of his pocket in a neat roll. Back then $1,000 was $1,000, too!

Debbie, being only three, dined with her grandmother every night while we had a second cocktail. The van stopped at each garden apartment, made the circle, and deposited whoever had gotten on at the main dining room of the hotel and then made the circuit again. This confused my daughter, who kept saying, "You're going to miss the bus!  Hurry!"

One night while Debbie and her Nana were in the dining room, Nana asked what she was going to eat that night. Debbie, in her best grown up voice, and picking up the menu that was upside down, said, "I think I'll just look at the menu first." The waiter loved it!

We all enjoyed the beach and the clear turquoise water so much. I perched on a big rock and observed so many beautiful fish swimming just about a foot under the clear water.

On this trip I was able to purchase some lovely British wool to bring back and have our seamstress make Debbie a beautiful pink and gray winter coat and leggings.

Many years later we made a third trip to Bermuda with club members of an organization my husband belonged to. This time we stayed at the other end of the island at Castle Harbor that felt so very different. While there we had a golf game at the very British Tucker's Town which is a gem!  The water views were so inspiring. Our golf cart broke down; however, and that was a huge problem for my husband. He marched into the pro shop declaring, "Not only am I not going to pay for my round of golf, but you're going to pay me since that cart broke down!"

That was our last trip to Bermuda.

# Portugal

We embarked on another trip that was quite enjoyable.

We arrived in Lisbon and went hurriedly to the hotel so we could get some sightseeing in before the party that night. We hailed a taxi after a short walk, and gestured wildly so that the driver got the idea that we wanted him to show us the sights. We saw beautiful parts of town and nice views of the Atlantic. There were very narrow alleys in the old (Algarve) section and the fruit, vegetable, meat and fish vendors had their wares out on tables in the sun. I saw flies on the fish and thought "ugh." I wondered how sanitary it was to shop like that. The displays were colorful, though, and would have made a very bright and cheery painting with red fish and green and yellow vegetables on those carts and tables.

Suddenly, we realized it was time to get back to our hotel. Now what was its name? We had no idea. I realized that we should have noted that before we left. (Note to self: in future, pick up matches off front desk or have clerk write name of hotel on note paper and hand it to you!) Now we had another tour of Lisbon

(Lisboa), one in which we drove to every hotel until we hit ours! Phew! It was about number eleven!

That evening we were treated to a sumptuous seafood buffet in a castle up very high that had a commanding view of the city with its narrow alleys and tile roof tops all the way to the ocean. It was a very glamorous setting for a delightful dinner party!

I went for an invigorating walk the next day up and down hilly streets. It was so interesting to see a man whip open his black coat and show me that inside, carefully arranged in the lining he had a collection of watches for sale. He whipped his heavy coat closed when he saw someone approach from another direction.

I strolled past the many foods that the vendors had out on tables again—lots of enormous fish were on display and the bright red ones really caught my eye. I browsed through the small shops and ended up in an appealing pub opening into the alley. I perched on a bar stool and ordered a beer so I could watch the parade go by.

The Portuguese people were very dark, swarthy and short in stature—some were bent over which made them appear even shorter. The predominant color of their apparel was black, black, and more black. They had a very happy nature and always smiled at us so we felt welcome.

That evening we went to a famous seafood restaurant near the water and I cheerfully ordered lobster. My husband almost fainted when he saw the bill, but I had reasoned that the ocean was just across the street so with such close proximity they must be plentiful and cheap. Wrong. Oh well. It was a very good dinner.

We went on a marvelous bus tour the next day up the sea coast. We were blessed with good weather and the villages sparkled in the sun. Sintra was a lovely spot full of story book homes by the sea and a wonderful castle with brightly colored walls—emerald green, powder blue, and yellow. After touring it we dispersed to a restaurant in Sintra for lunch. I had a fairly easy time translating European menus as Romance languages are related and I had had three years of French and two of Latin. Of course, there is some differentiation as "potage" is the word for "soup" in French, but it becomes "sopa" in other countries. That word looks a lot like "soup" anyway. Well, my dad had told me before our trip to always order soup because they are masters at making it in Europe. He said that they had enormous pots in which they let ingredients simmer continually. I ordered cabbage soup, therefore, and the others at our table laughed at the idea. When it arrived, it was very creamy and smelled heavenly and they all wanted some!

We proceeded next to a gambling town on the coast called Estoril. It cost $10.00 to go into the casino but I really wanted to so I talked my husband into it. (He was still smarting from the lobster dinner.) It was a magical place. The entrance was very impressive with elegantly attired people milling about. In the far corner of the casino was a long table with an elbow rest two feet above the green felt surface and a group of women with long dresses and very white gloves to the elbow and men in tuxedos were playing chemin de fer there and resting their elbows on the leather rail above the table. Others were playing card games. I changed my bills into coins (called "escudos") and hit the slots. Believe it or not, I hit a jackpot and all those little dime-sized coins came crashing down onto the floor! There were so many so I started to scramble around and pick them up when I noticed the sophisticated gamblers at the chemin de fer table turn their heads and stare disapprovingly at me! Hurriedly I scooped them up and ran to the desk in the lobby to cash them in. Well, their value was equivalent to "tuppence" in England or pennies in the US! Darn! So much for instant riches!

That night we had a special treat in store. We were going to a popular restaurant for dinner and would get to see the "fado." This is a beautiful dance that has all the drama of the tango. This very professional floor show was put on by one couple dressed in deep black who seemed to be together and then apart with so much facial and bodily expression of love, anger, hurt—the whole range of human emotions. Unfortunately, one of the tables of American tourists was noisy so the waiter reprimanded them and explained that this was a very expensive restaurant for the Portugese people who would save all year to come here on their anniversary or birthday to enjoy their native dance!

They also entertained us with a very good quartet who sang "April in Portugal." In those days we had 33 RPM records so I bought one and love it.

On a sour note, most of our group went shopping in a particular store during our visit and one of the orthodontists asked the clerk behind the counter if the jewelry he was examining represented one of the native crafts of SPAIN! We were in Portugal! The clerk was hurt by the question, of course. The small country is proud of its history and not overly friendly with Spain, a much larger country that borders it.

# Spain

We took a short flight to Madrid and arrived at the very glamorous Melia Castellia Hotel, which bowled me over. They were serving Sangria in the lobby, for one thing, and I've never to this day had any to compare with it—the real Spanish Sangria!

Also in the lobby was posted a huge sign so that we would know where to gather when we needed to get on a tour bus. The sign read, "Fairfax County Dental Association." This really confused everyone else because they had never heard of "Fairfax County" and didn't know what to make of us.

Our room was a little slice of heaven and ahead of its time in the features it boasted. It was quite large, first of all, and boasted three or four phones. It had the first refrigerator I had seen in a hotel room back in 1970. It had a beautiful Louis XIV desk and huge king-sized beds.

We were treated to a tour of the world-famous Prado Museum featuring masterpieces by Valazquez, Goya, and El Greco. I could have spent more time there, but our group wasn't as interested in art as I was!

We also saw the very impressive Royal Palace of

Madrid which no longer houses the Royal Family, but is used for state occasions. The rooms open for the tour numbered about 27 which is a fraction of the total number. (3,418 rooms!) Still, it was a large number to go through and the decorating and furniture were stunning! It, too, is a treasure house of art.

I was prepared to have a wonderful dinner at the famous Horcher Restaurant and what I recall most vividly is the fact that they brought footstools to all of us which made us feel important! That, and the fact that instead of the spicy food I was anticipated, it was bland and even needed salt! And everywhere we went they had that boring, bland dessert, flan.

The next night we descended on a very different, fun restaurant called "Da Meo Patacca" which I think means, "Of my uncle." I still have the enormous menu on the wall of my den. This restaurant is under the streets and has interesting caverns, candles and Spanish music. It was a lot of fun!

I observed that many well-dressed Spanish ladies were on street corners awaiting public transportation. They wore black cocktail dresses and suits and black heels. I learned that so many live in town in rather small apartments so they go out to meet friends and eat dinner.

In those days there were other people on street corners—armed guards carrying guns. After our country in those days, this filled us with fear as something we had never seen before! I clearly remember being thankful that we didn't have to live like that!

Soon it was time to continue our journey through Spain. We headed to Valle de los Caidos. (Valley of the Fallen). This is a truly incredible sight, unlike any other. Here we saw a great cross (500 foot) visible from the air, over the entrance to a huge underground church commissioned by General Francesco Franco to celebrate his victory in the Spanish Civil War. The entrance is actually into a mountain, near its top. There is no other place like this. It's also cold, dark, and damp and started me on the way to fever and chills.

We then toured Toledo, which is a very interesting ancient city. It was breathtaking to enter because we did so over a bridge built by the Romans in 11th century, we were told, with the actual stone gateway being from the Arab period of the 9th century! To that date I had never seen anything that old and I was so impressed! The huge medieval stone walls surrounded the city and inside the streets and alleys were too narrow to permit cars so all sightseeing was on foot.

Toledo has several claims to fame, the first being

metal craftsmanship, so my husband bought a huge sword which hung in our den.

El Greco (The Greek) lived here so we toured his home and heard a description of his life. He was a very talented and famous painter, of course, and his masterpieces were not only on display there but in many churches and convents in Toledo as well as in a special museum. The long, sad faces which are easily recognizable as his art were often painted of people from the insane asylum, which I thought very interesting.

We separated from the group as I had heard of a very good restaurant there and wanted to try it. I was a little concerned about what time we had to meet our group at the gate so I asked the waiter about "the gate," which is "la porte" in most romance languages, so when I said "porte" to the waiter, pointing to my watch, he thought I meant port wine and started hauling out bottles of it from the kitchen. We found a waiter who could speak French so I found out how long a walk it was from there to the gate.

We had a friend in Madrid who was a sister of our neighbor in Staunton. She had ended up there in a most interesting way:  she went on a trip to Madrid and liked it so much that she was determined to find work she could do so she could stay. Also, she didn't know a word of Spanish, so that had to be learned.

I had asked her, "But Sarah!  How did you know what to order in restaurants?"

She said, "I didn't, and sometimes I had some very strange food."

Back in those pre-internet days, she hit on a plan to teach med students English so they could read our advanced medical journals and articles. They would go to her apartment for lessons.

After returning from our travels out of town back to Madrid my husband called her number. She answered in Spanish, of course, and their greeting was something like "Okay, you called me so start talking," instead of "hello." We were laughing and then she knew who it was, so we could speak English.

My husband told her that I was sick in bed with fever and chills so she got a doctor for me and took my husband shopping. What a trooper!  How do you repay favors like that!  He had a pattern with him that she could change from English measurements to Spanish, for the clerk, and more beautiful material for an evening gown was then purchased.

I was weak as a kitten that day but the rest saved my life and I was able to fly home the next day.

# France and England

In 1970 Mother called and invited me to join my grandmother, father, and herself for part of a wonderful European trip they were planning to take in April.

In those days you could make an appointment with a travel agent and customize your travel experience rather than take a standard tour.

My father, a man of great imagination, seized this opportunity with heart and soul and kept reading and planning and probably drove the travel agent to a breakdown with his new ideas and changes!

My grandmother had originally thought that a trip to the Hawaiian Islands would be wonderful, but my parents were much more interested in the history and art treasures of Europe and England so she went along with that idea.

My parents had been to Europe to celebrate Mother's birthday and were anxious to return. During this trip they flew over the Swiss Alps, which was breathtaking, and suddenly the stewardess came down the aisle with glasses of champagne for everyone. She said, "It's the pilot's birthday!" My father spoke up and said, "It's my wife's birthday, too!"

The stewardess reported this to the pilot who then invited them up to the cockpit so they could see even more scenery and congratulate each other! Mother was so touched by this that all she could say was, "This is a long way from Cass County!" (Her Indiana birthplace).

On this same trip they were touring Italy when they ran out of film so they purchased some there. Tragically, none of the pictures they took there turned out with that film!

When I accepted the invitation to join them for part of their tour in 1970, I was so excited! They had many adventures before I met up with them and I can remember some of what they told me.

They had a marvelous time in Austria because they had a dear friend there, Hugo Stowasse, whom they had met in America years before and he was to meet them and show them around. He delighted in this and they had a great time. Mother said that the streets were either "gasses" or "strasses" (alleys or streets) and that some of the palaces were beautiful; in fact, they were staying in one which had become a hotel and it was gorgeous with its huge crystal chandeliers and marble floors and walls, lovely Oriental rugs were everywhere.

The first night they were in residence there my grandmother got up to go into the bathroom, but the

Oriental rug by her bed slipped on the marble floor so she fell backwards, hitting her head on the side board of her bed with a sharp blow.

Looking in the bathroom mirror she saw blood pouring out of the back of her head. Not wanting to disturb Mother and Dad, she elevated her head on the propped-up pillow and thought that stemmed the flow of blood.

In the morning she arose and dressed and combed her hair but in so doing, tore the scab and the blood flowed quite freely. She then called Mother up and when she saw my grandmother she was terribly worried and called the desk. The clerk said that he would call a cab immediately to take everyone to the hospital.

They all climbed in, my grandmother holding a large handkerchief against the wound, and the cab driver said that he would turn on the siren to make better headway against the traffic. Then he proceeded to screech around corners at full speed and drive up and over sidewalks to get by cars.

This alarmed by grandmother so much that she yelled, "Please slow down! I'd rather bleed to death than be killed in a traffic accident!"

This struck my parents as very funny, so they got the giggles.

The cab driver then turned around and admonished them sharply, shouting, "Don't laugh! When the siren is on, you must look very serious!"

This of course, made them all giggle harder!

Eventually they reached the hospital and Nana was stitched and clamped and told that they must check into the hospitals in each port of call to make sure it was healing properly. This added interest to their European tour since not every doctor spoke English!

Meanwhile, I was preparing to meet them in Paris. My mother-in-law was moving into our house to take care of my four-year-old daughter, and my husband drove me to the local airport for the connector to Dulles Airport. He glared at me, but it didn't spoil my happiness.

All I could think about was that it was Earth Day (April 22) and my plane was leaving the earth!

I had a lot of time to kill in the Dulles Airport, but I was so excited about finally getting to see Paris (a dream since studying French in high school) that I couldn't concentrate on the book I had brought. I kept having flashbacks to my class room at Shortridge High School and the map of the streets of Paris which was always unrolled over a section of the backboard and my teacher in her neat dark green suit, saying, "Some day you will go there" and my thinking, I doubt it! Well I smiled and thought of Gertrude M. Weathers and wished she knew. Maybe she did.

I had to express myself so I started talking to a nice family. I asked where they were going and they said "Oklahoma." I said, "Oh, that's nice." I thought, Oh, you poor people!

We boarded Air France around 7 PM (we kiddingly called it "Air Chance"). I was so excited. I ate and drank everything they served. About midnight I tried to sleep, but if I did, it was very little! The stewardesses were always offering something and finally gave us rolled up hot, scented hand towels to refresh us. Love the French!

I found out later that my parents had a bet as to what I would do that first day in Paris! We landed in the early morning and their plane wasn't due until 3 or 4 in the afternoon (Paris time). Mother thought I would try to catch up on my sleep and wait for them in the safety of the hotel. My Dad was just as sure that I would be so excited that I would go exploring right away. All I can say is, he won the bet.

I couldn't wait to use my best French on the cab driver. There was just one problem; I wanted the Rue de Castile which we pronounce "cas-teel" but it

sounds very different with the French pronunciation
of "Cas-tee-yuh." I finally wrote it down and was safely
delivered to the right address.

Mother had enjoyed picking the perfect hotel in the
perfect location! It was small, charming, authentically
French (owned by a French family – not a boring
American chain) and it was across the side street
from the fabulous Ritz that fronted on The Place de
Vendome, known the world over for its chic shops. The
Ritz would be handy when we wanted a fancy bar and
to people watch. (In those days we could move about
freely. Now you have to be a guest of most nice hotels
to gain entrance).

I paid the driver in francs. (This was before Euros).
I remember that there were 5 francs to 1 dollar so I
thought of them as 20 cent pieces. Still, it looked like
Monopoly money and I had to remind myself that it
was serious cash! I was delighted with the hotel and
enjoyed speaking French! I entered a small, inviting
dining room with little French antique chairs. Behind
it was a very cozy bar with five or six stools. In Europe
I learned they were small and such a pleasant place to
have a nightcap after a big night out. On the left a
semi-circular wooden, narrow staircase wound around
a mini scale elevator—big enough for two or three

persons! I had to laugh—instead of a "down" button a button said, "en bas." Mom and I laughed over that later. It was pretty scary, but I had big suitcases so I took this little elevator to the second floor, left my suitcases, and took off!

I could not wait! Paris! I was in Paris! I walked and walked, observing everything! There was a magazine stand with a magazine called "Les Parents," (French edition of Parents' Magazine). There were odd-looking circular metal stalls every several blocks called "Pissoirs" for men to relieve themselves without being seen.

There was a couple working the streets with a camera who approached me, offering to take a picture of me in Paris. In broken English they asked where I was from in America. (I was obviously an American). They guessed "California." Foreigners have heard of California! I said, "No, Virginia." They pretended to have heard of it. The woman asked for Travelers' Checques and proceeded to pat her hand on my purse! What nerve! I shrieked and ran away.

Next I found a department store called "Au Printemps." Translation: "Spring". I was happily wandering through it in search of a beautiful French stylish frock for my four-year-old. Unfortunately I was unable to find one.

Suddenly, I decided to look for a Ladies' Room but didn't see one, so I asked a lovely looking lady behind one of the counters for what I thought was the right wording: "Ou est la salle de bain?" (Where is the bathroom?) She guided me to the bath department in the store and began pulling out washcloths and towels. I said, "Non, non, la salle de bain," accompanied by a worried expression. She burst out laughing and said, "Oh, la toilette!" This they never taught us in French class! Oh, well, I made her day. By the way, it became "toiletta" in Italian.

Finally, the lack of sleep and the long flight began to get to get to me so I hightailed it back to my small, French hotel, chanced the rickety elevator again and fell into a nice, hot bathtub, and the bed.

At 3:30 (Paris time) in came my relatives, full of smiles and happiness! I was so glad to see them! Nana and I were sharing a room right below Mother and Dad's. My parents were only 58 and 59 then and raring to go! We went to the concierge downstairs to get suggestions and have him make our reservations. He was a very jolly Frenchman and took great delight in making us love his city! That first night, however, we were going to one of my godmother's favorite restaurants. (She was the French teacher who had escaped Omaha and moved to Paris and given Mother a list of her favorite restaurants and shops before my parents left the U.S.)

The concierge called this restaurant for us "l'Auberge de la Truite" ("The Inn of the Trout" in English.) We set off on foot and discovered this darling place down an alley and had the most superb trout dinner I've ever had! Back then what Mother said was completely true: "You can't go to a bad restaurant in France. They're all just wonderful!" That was before today's fast food invasion and before restaurants of many other cultures came.

Now when I pause to recollect that magic time in "The City of Lights," I see before me a veritable storm of red, white and blue confetti and I hear a concertina and there's a red windmill turning on the roof of The Moulin Rouge!

One day I went to the fabulous Louvre Museum with Dad, cheerfully climbing a great staircase up to the Statue of Winged Victory and then down the great hall to a room on the right where we could gaze at The Mona Lisa. This, like Broadway and Wall Street, or anything you've heard of just forever, I expected it to be huge and was pretty disappointed that it was so small, just as I had been with the other two I named.

We spent a lot of time there as we both loved art,

and Dad knew some fascinating stories behind many paintings there.

That evening we were excited about going on a ride down the beautiful Seine on a boat called, the "Bateau Mouche" which would glide right by Notre Dame and cruise for several hours through the magically lit Paris at night!

We boarded carefully and were seated in the cabin with lots of windows at a lovely table set for dinner with a white linen cloth and napkins, silver and nine wine glasses! I could see that we were to be very busy!

To make it complete, a smiling Frenchman came strolling by our table playing a concertina! There has never been such a magnificent dinner! We had a delicious course to go with each wine glass!

After this uniquely enchanting evening, we poured ourselves into a taxi and couldn't wait to tell our concierge/bartender back at our small hotel about how wonderful it all was, over a nightcap, of course!

The next day we took a wonderful walk down The Rive Gauche (The Left Bank), famous for its artists, bookstalls, lovers and students, old inns and taverns—just the most romantic place on earth. We decided to have dinner there because Dad told us about a restaurant there he had known in his youth called "Roger le Grenouille" (Roger the Frog) which specialized in frog legs. My grandmother's favorite food was probably frog legs so she was enthusiastic. Dad said it was very informal so he didn't know if we would like it. We loved it!  We sat at long tables filled with French students who were singing boisterously— all their school songs at the top of their lungs!  Over our heads we were passing enormous round trays laden with frog legs!  We caught on to some of the words in the choruses, so we joined right in the singing. It was a very memorable evening with a different, fun vibe!

The following day I decided to call my old boyfriend and see if we could get together and reminisce for old time's sake. This turned out to be a huge adventure! At that time, I had to go to this big building and ask for help (in French!) to find his phone number, not only because there were so many phone directories in this building but also because they were arranged by categories I didn't know about. It was bewildering and I had no idea if he even lived in France or in Paris at that time. I had dated him in college when he was a student at Washington and Lee University in Lexington, Virginia when he had come there from Nancy in Alsace – Lorraine, but I knew that he wanted to work in Paris.

The nice little Frenchman with whom I communicated in my faltering French grinned with delight!  His eyes really lit up at the idea and he plunged into several big, heavy directories before emerging, triumphant from this enormous search with the right one in his hand! Then he kind of hung around after dialing the number for me. He was grinning from ear-to-ear as I spoke hesitantly in French. Jean-Marie sounded delighted and said he could pick me up at my hotel and take me to his home to meet his family and have a "quick lunch" (pronounced 'queek') and then tour Versailles if I would like that!  Would I like that?"  I'll say.

I told my family that I wouldn't be with them on Sunday and why, and they got a kick out of the plan. They had wonderful plans for that day themselves involving a fabulous brunch and people-watching at a very, very nice hotel.

Jean-Marie arrived at the appointed hour, handsome as ever with some gray hair at the temples and very well dressed in a business suit. He entered the pretty hotel parlor and was glad to see my parents again and to meet my grandmother.

Then we stepped outside and Jean-Marie laughed about the dog in the street barking in French  and about forgetting the English word for cul-de-sac and

I told him that people who spoke English usually used the French expression "cul-de-sac," but I thought he meant, "dead end" which we also say. He was delighted to hear that expression again. Long story short, it was as if time had stood still and we were young and laughing together again, although both married to others now and both with a family. Somehow time just melted away in that small French car as we sped towards his home.

Upon entering I was greeted warmly by his wife, Anne, (The French pronounce it "Ahn," which is softer) and their two adorable children who were beautifully dressed and very well behaved. They were very polite and endured a very long day with adults! We were ushered into the living room and cocktails were offered, but nothing I had ever seen before. I believe we drank Campari, which, as Mother said later, is a very strange drink to our palates—very bitter! I sipped daintily and didn't care for it at all.

Then Jean-Marie decided to wind up his ancient Victrola and put a record on and he chose the Washington and Lee marching song! When he started singing along I joined in and suddenly I burst into tears! I was so embarrassed and mystified at the same time! I still have absolutely no idea why that happened but I almost couldn't stop! I have never been more embarrassed!

The table was set at the other end of the room with places for all of us so we sat down as I wiped my eyes. I wonder what those children thought!

Anne brought out a lovely large silver tray bedecked with cold cuts of all kinds. They were artistically arranged along with cheeses (France produces hundreds of different cheeses). I exclaimed, "Oh, how nice! This is just the right amount of food for lunch! Everywhere we go people to try to give us too much food!"

Big faux pas! In my eagerness to be polite, I said just the wrong thing. Course after course after course was brought in from the kitchen! I'll bet there were a dozen courses! "Queek lunch," my eye! Not where I come from.

The children who were more like miniature adults than children, endured it all, sat through it, and never interrupted.

Anne spoke English pretty well, having summered once with a relative in England, so she kept up her end of the conversation. Once she was talking about a neighbor and seemed stumped because she couldn't think of the English word. She said, "You know—a house for the horses." I offered, "Barn?" She was very relieved and continued her tale.

At last we were ready to leave the groaning board (after the second dessert!) and head for Versailles. The children were included at that time in Europe; this was often the case. I didn't notice baby sitters (of course, England had many, many nannies).

Versailles was quite close to the house and was magnificent, of course! Outside this lovely French castle was a miniature farm complete with cows, lamb, barns—the works. Jean-Marie explained that Marie Antoinette loved to play at farming!

We entered the castle and had a French guide, so the entire tour was in French and spoken faster than I could keep up with; consequently, Jean-Marie had to explain almost everything that was just said to me. As a result, all I really remember was that there was a hidden door in the wall next to the headboard of the royal bed, through which the King could sneak into the room of his mistress. I also recall the elaborate painting, decorating, and Louis IV furniture and how hard it was to study the paintings where all these other things were vying for your attention.

At one point their little boy whispered to his father who tried to "shush" him, but the poor little tyke just wanted to know where the bathroom was! I kept contrasting these little angels with American children the same age and simply could not imagine such adult behavior by Americans!

Comparing notes with my family after this wonderful Sunday I was happy that they had loved their brunch and people-watching in a very sophisticated location. Oh, Paris!

The next evening was quite thrilling as we were going to dine at the world famous restaurant, La Tour d'Argent (The Silver Tower), so we took our baths earlier than usual so we could devote much time to dressing up. Mother and I were both talking as we bathed – she to my Father in their adjoining bedroom, and I to my grandmother, also in our adjoining bed chamber

Suddenly Mother cried out, "Judy?"

I heard her so clearly above me and so I answered, "Yes!  I can hear you."

We discovered that our voices were traveling up and down the adjoining wall as the floor above didn't quite meet it!  That was the oddest thing!  So we cheerfully discussed what we were going to wear as we each sat in our bathtubs!

I had mentioned that we were going to La Tour d'Argent to Jean-Marie and he responded, "Ah, le canard!" which is French for "The Duck."

Soon we were off and, once there, noticed that we had to enter an outside elevator. We were deposited into a very charming, large room, with windows all along the front overlooking a magnificent view of the gently flowing Seine replete with bateaux mouches gliding by to light up the exterior of the Cathedral of Notre Dame with its magnificent rose window and flying buttresses. It was one of the most dramatic subjects I've ever seen, especially from that height.

The waiter took us to a table in back with absolutely no view at which moment my father came unglued and expostulated in a loud voice, "We came to eat here in order to enjoy the view!  We will NOT sit back in this corner!"

The waiter looked very upset and hastily led us to an excellent table right next to a window. And that's all I remember about that evening!  I have no idea if I had "le canard."

We had a favorite stop in the afternoons in Paris. Watlings Red Ale was what the sign inside said, and we would drop in for a beer and chat. About the third time we did so the owner served us and one minute later announced it was closing time so we would have to drink up!  This was when we realized that many of the French disliked Americans.

Another day I was walking around by myself, dressed up as we did in those days with heels and a suit, when a French lady approached me and asked me in French, of course, where something was. I was so flattered to have looked French and not glaringly American!

Mother had her hair done and it was the prettiest hairdo I ever saw her have, softer, with ringlets. Dad and I thought she looked very French and lovely.

One evening we closed up Harrys' American Bar! I don't know how many after dinner drinks we had but several! We laughed because the piano player, though playing Gershwin, had no feel for the rhythm and just kept reading notes and giving them all the same value, which made it hard to identify the song at times.

The next morning Mother called down from her bathtub and said she was afraid she had left her glasses there so I ran over there—it wasn't too far—and asked in my best French. The bartender reached next to the cash register and handed them to me. Mother was so relieved!

That day we had a very elegant lunch at The Cafe de la Paix (Cafe of Peace). It's very well known, near our hotel and across from the opera house. My father had a strong urge to see an opera but, after, racing up the many steps, found that they were sold out. (Mother heaved a sigh of relief). She had been so afraid she would have to sit through that.

On our last night we did the real tourist thing of seeing the Moulin Rouge complete with the can can, food served to our theatre seats, and dancing. It was lots of fun and everyone should see it while there. A nice-looking man asked me to dance, but I refused thinking I shouldn't as a married woman. My relatives urged me to because it would be fun and what was the harm, but I felt guilty about leaving when my husband was mad and hardly spoke when he took me to the plane. I guess he laid a real guilt trip on me. Silly!

The next day we would be off for London! It was a short plane ride that turned into a long one as we had to circle and circle Heathrow. The word was that we were stacked up and awaiting our turn. I have never been a good flier so I was talking to my grandmother about anything else when I saw the tail of a plane peeking through the clouds very close to us. It looked close enough to touch to me! At last we darted down and landed! I was never so glad to land before or since!

Now we had to wait in line at customs in Heathrow. This was my very first taste of how very kind and considerate the British are! As we stood in line, a kind gentleman came up on the other side of the rope and beckoned to my grandmother offering her a chair.

I said, "Hey, I'm with her," just kiddingly, and he responded, "I'm sorry but this is for privileged persons only." Nana just beamed and smiled.

That was where their kindness first showed itself and it never stopped! It made me so proud to be of English descent, and yet somewhat humble because Americans, for the most part aren't as courteous and thoughtful constantly!

We collected our bags and made our way to the taxi area, looking for Clark's Limousines. Nana and my parents had arranged for them to meet us and we spotted them in a long black limo with "Clark" on top. They had top hats!  Besides the driver there was another gentleman assigned to assist us and he also sat in front. There was a sliding glass partition on top of the front seats that reached to the ceiling that they delicately closed, telling us to rap on the glass if we had any questions. Mother laughed, "Nothing so delicate as to hear our conversations!"

We began our drive to our London hotel and looked out of the windows with great interest, having never been to England before. What we saw were modest small homes with small, neat yards, each one the exact same size and quite level, and each one sporting window boxes with the most cheerful blooms you can imagine—bright reds and blues, yellow and with blossoms. Many had tiny flower gardens as well as those square back yards. My, the English certainly did love their flowers!

We talked among ourselves and presently thought of a question so we "rapped on the glass." A gray gloved hand in the front seat slid it open and so we said, "Excuse me, but is there shopping near our hotel?"

The answer was our first delicious taste of British humor. The answer came back, "Rawther too close for the gentleman, I'm sure."

I don't know who writes their material, but it's always delivered with a straight face and twinkling eyes! We laughed ourselves silly.

At last we pulled up at the Mayfair. Our driver said that this was a very popular hotel with Americans.

I loved the location—a park-like setting in a busy city. There were trees, benches, and a lovely green space across from it, rectangular in shape. Later I learned that it was Berkeley Square. Mother, who had a beautiful voice, started singing, "and a nightingale sang in Berkeley Square." She knew all the words and it certainly fit the bucolic scene.

We found a cheerful bellboy who somehow managed

all our suitcases with very good cheer. Awaiting the elevator, we noticed beautiful tall brass ashtrays with engraving on them that read "cigarette ends." Mother said, "Nothing so indelicate as 'butts.'"

I loved Nana's and my room—big and airy and, wonder of wonders, it had the most marvelous brass tubular heated towel racks in the bathroom! I've never had that luxury before or since!

I cheerfully explored and enjoyed the huge, floor to ceiling, closet with heavy wooden doors and some built-in drawers that were labeled. One mystified me. The label read "jumpers." I wondered why you would put a jumper in a drawer.

We bathed and changed and hurried down to enjoy the bar atmosphere, but we had to wait. Why? Because tea time is sacred to the British and during those hours you can only get tea, don't you know. They also have very lovely round-tiered tea trays laden with delicacies guaranteed to spoil your dinner.

As we sat in the lobby waiting for the magic hour when the bar would open, my father came over to us laughing. He said that he had been in so many countries with so many languages that he had gone up to the desk there in the lobby, forming in his mind just how to ask the clerk in French for a weekly paper that advertised what plays and concerts were going on while we were there and when he reached the desk another man came up and started talking to the clerk in English! Dad had laughed then and realized that he could ask for it in English! He was quite happy.

The only play he could get last minute tickets for starred Jerry Lewis, of all people, but it was a chance to see their famous Theatre district, Soho, so we jumped at it. It was pretty amusing and always fun to go to the theatre!

The next day I decided to go on a mission and Mother wanted to go on one of her own, so we split up. Mother wanted to add to some of her china that was hard to get but was made there, so with address in hand she set out. The only problem was, the numbers were not consecutive so they were very confusing! Everyone in England is so nice so she asked a lady on that street if she could help. Mother said that the lady was stumped, too, but just determined to be helpful. When at last they gave up, Mother said that she left that lady on the street corner, shaking her head and saying, "Oh, I'm so terribly, terribly sorry!"

Meanwhile I set out to find a jumper for Debbie in the Armstrong plaid, since that was her surname. I couldn't wait to see what it looked like and to tell her about it if I could find it.

As I crossed streets I was very impressed with the number of cast iron statues in the shape of dogs, cats, and children that were almost life size and painted gaily. Upon inspection I saw that each represented a charity and there was a place to insert coins—every charity known to man such as blind dogs, deaf cats, orphans, and I can't begin to remember what all. All I could think was if I ever run out of money in Europe, please, Lord, let it be in England. They will take care of me. I love those people.

There was a lot of traffic where the cab deposited me and Harrods, the world famous department store, was right in front of me, with the Scotch House diagonally across the street. I couldn't wait to see them both so I first went into Harrods which had a fancy announcement in the window that read, "By appointment to Her Majesty, the Queen" with her coat-of-arms. I learned that if she wants to shop, the store is then closed to everyone else.

Upon gaining entrance I was "blown away" by a huge, "ginormous" flower show that seemed to go on forever. Beautiful blooms as far as you could see! My, that was a huge store!

They had an immense fancy food and tea section

on the main floor as well. I ascended in the "lift" (not "elevator" in England!) and enjoyed browsing on several floors. There was a large carved crystal panel with different wonderful sayings about England such as "There will always be an England," "When a man is tired of London, he is tired of Life" by Samuel Johnson. I kept thinking, How True!

Presently I tore myself away and started trying to cross the large busy street to the Scotch House.

A very nice lady came over to wait on me. I explained that I was interested in getting the Armstrong plaid for my daughter and did they have a jumper? She gave me a rather odd look, disappeared and reappeared, carrying two cardigan sweaters!

I said, "No! Those are sweaters!"

She answered, "We call them jumpers."

I said, well, that explains the drawer in my closet at the hotel that's labeled "jumpers". Then I described the article of clothing I wanted with cut outs for the blouse sleeves and she intoned in her British accent, "Oh, a petticoat dress!"

I told Mother later and she said, "Oh, the language barrier again!"

That evening we decided on the Caprice restaurant, having been advised not to eat English cooking but rather to eat in foreign restaurants in London. We thought we couldn't go wrong with a French restaurant, and it wasn't far from the hotel. Were we ever right! It was a superb French restaurant and we adored everything. For dessert I thought it would be fun to order the "Surprise Caprice" so I asked the waiter what it was and he grinned and said, "Oh, it's a surprise!" I ordered it, of course, and it was so heavenly that here I am writing about it 47 years later! It was the first and only baked Alaska I've ever had and it was perfection itself, with home-made chocolate sauce drizzled down the front and ice cream inside a beautiful pastry shell.

After our delectable repast we thought of calling a cab since it was raining slightly, so, huddled under the canopy outside, we saw two handsome, tall Englishmen walk by with their omni-present black umbrellas firmly tucked under their arms, saying to each other, "It isn't a bit bad really!"

So we felt like sissies and decided to walk. I asked the doorman where the Mayfair was from there and he took me by the elbow and walked halfway down the block with me until he was positive that I could see it. I could only contrast that with how it would have been in America—the doorman saying, "Oh, it's over that way" and pointing and then turning away.

Of course, we had a nightcap in the bar with all those handsome British gentlemen. My Father "had his roller skates on" as Mother would say and was making all sorts of acquaintances. One was especially interesting to him and he wanted to hear all of his sad story about wages and taxes in England, so Mother went to bed and had to leave the room unlocked because there was only one key for some reason. Dad stayed up half the night! Sometimes he went a little wild.

It was cold in England in April! In fact, I had one heavy, thick wool suit with me (we didn't wear slacks in those days) that I kept putting on almost every day as it was so heavy and warm. It was navy and emerald green and I loved the colors, but I really got tired of it!

I decided to tour the Victoria and Albert Museum on my own, spend some time there, and then just explore. I couldn't leave! They had entire parlors and bedrooms set up with authentic fabric, wallpaper and furniture as well as many magnificent paintings, statues, and just everything imaginable from that period. I did break away very briefly to get some lunch at a pub nearby with really dark bitter beer, "A pint of beer please," and Scotch eggs. These are hard boiled eggs that have been messed with and sitting in a giant jar on the bar. I felt I had to do the "when in England, do as the English do" thing so I did. I could cheerfully live the rest of my life without them.

One thing we were really looked forward to was touring the Tower of London, checking out the Beefeater soldiers who stand at perfect attention and won't look at you, hearing all the fascinating details about the beheading of Henry VIII's wives and their tortuous imprisonment in the tower, and reveling in the gloom and dark and dampness. On the brighter side, we sat perfectly still and gazed upon either the crown jewels or paste substitutes. No one knew for sure. Whatever they were, they were safely encased behind thick Plexiglas walls. Mother was thrilled and wanted to believe that they were real!

After this show was over we found a ladies' room and, upon entering, were once again aware of the kind hearts possessed by the English people: There was a place in each door to deposit coins to unlock it, except for two stalls which didn't require any money. They were labeled, "Pregnant Woman."

There was a store nearby selling Dickens memorabilia so I went in. Everywhere you looked there was something interesting. That day we also toured Westminster Abbey with its famous Poets' Corner. It's a beautiful cathedral, architecturally perfect, and makes one want to just hush and drink it all in.  So much pomp and circumstance has taken place here. I loved reading the names of the poets buried here.

We also climbed up, up, up to St. Paul's. It has a magnificent view of part of London and is a lovely church. For some reason I remember how overcome by emotion Mother was and how she donated money as a loyal Episcopalian.

The oddest thing about London, I thought, was that wherever we were going, we always ended up at Trafalgar Square, a monument to Lord Horatio Nelson who won the Battle of Trafalgar. There is a very tall column dedicated to him, but the whole thing is a large area with statues of lions. It seems to be where roads cross that you want and you just always end up saying, "Here we are again."  I recently read that it was being worked on so traffic had to avoid it and I wondered how in the world you could!

We also took in the stirring ceremony of the changing of the guard at Windsor Castle. Tourists line up and crowd around to see this perfect ceremony, some of us climbing up a bit on the status of Queen Victoria in order to see it better. That woman was certainly no beauty, which the huge statue plainly illustrates.

One of the most outstanding memories of London

was my trip to the famous store, Fortnum and Mason. There is absolutely nothing like the ceremony that occurred there every hour. On the balcony overlooking the first floor stood a small brass clock in the center. Every hour on the hour it would chime the hour and from the wings two bewigged gentlemen in knee breeches and elegant silk coats appeared. They walked towards each other and, taking turns, signed the same agreement of their partnership that the original Mr. Fortnum and Mr. Mason signed on a desk with quill pens under the brass clock. Then they shook hands and disappeared back into the wings.

I simply had to meet them and tell them how much I loved their store and their ceremony. Mr. Fortnum's descendant then asked me where I was from and I answered, "Virginia". He smiled and said, "Oh, the Colonies!"

I went upstairs for high tea and was very pleased that everyone else there seemed to be British and not a tourist. The tea service was just beautiful on a graduated tier of round plates with a brass rod running through their middle with a handle on top. The tiny cakes, sandwiches and beautifully decorated sweets were so gorgeous that I wanted to paint them before eating. I was surrounded by people speaking the English language so perfectly that it was a feast for the ears as well as the eyes!

Walking on air I hailed a cab and went back to the Mayfair to tell my family about this glorious foray into a fine British institution when we received a call form the front desk. They told us that our bill was ready if we wanted to settle it before leaving in the morning. We all panicked as we were sure it has been prepaid. The clerk at the desk said that it had not. (This was before credit cards). My grandmother started blaming herself for not having gotten a "letter of credit" from her bank. We called a meeting and everyone emptied their pockets on one of the double beds. We counted out how many pounds we had between us in a loud voice. All of a sudden, the phone beside the bed rang and it was the desk clerk. He said, "I've found the documentation with your reservation and you're right. You have paid ahead." We started cheering and tossing the pounds straight up into the air!

Mother was just jubilant and insisted that we take a cab to the Ritz Hotel to celebrate with a cocktail and that's exactly what we did! Of course that was the hotel back in Hemingway's time but many others have gained favor since the 40's and 50's so we had the elegant surroundings to ourselves. Nevertheless, we had a grand time.

The next morning, we went to Heathrow together, they to fly back home and I to fly to Rome where I would meet my husband who was already there for an orthodontists' meeting.

I sat next to a tall, dashing Englishman who started talking to me about how I liked London. What stands out to me is that he said, "You Americans make such long words out of perfectly good English words. For example, we have a perfectly good word, "transport" and you made it "transportation."

By George, he was right!

# Discovering the Orient

I certainly never would have gone to the Orient had I not received a phone call at my desk one March morning from a good friend who asked abruptly,

"Do you want to go to China?"

I said, "Sure, sure."

She answered, "Good! We have a Human Resource Directors' trip to China and Japan in October and I don't want to room with someone I've never met."

Well, it was March so it seemed safe enough to commit because October was a long way off and it might never get here.

I've never seen months fly faster! And each one brought a new request for a payment of some kind towards the trip.

The year was 1984 and we were called "trend setters." China had just opened to tourism perhaps the preceding year and was heavily regimented under Communist regulations. We were issued a book about China and instructions for the trip including the necessity of wearing jeans and dark colors in Northern China—nothing dressy—because the Chinese people at that time wore padded suits of either blue or gray and we were to "blend in." We were also told that we could bring tea bags as they had lots of thermoses of hot water and we would find tea bags useful. I thought to myself that I had never liked tea—reminded me of being sick in bed—so I had a bright idea of bringing bouillon cubes. We also had to pack a few nicer clothes for Hong Kong nightlife (very glamorous!) and Japan.

The great day for our trip was quickly at hand so we drove to Dulles where I vainly looked for an empty space in the "long term" lot. Seeing none, I parked in "short term." We laughed a lot—parking in "short term" when we were headed to the Orient for 3 weeks!

We wisely broke the very long trip by staying three days in L.A. before our flight to Tokyo. We had a grand time going to Sea World and seeing other touristy sites like movie stars' homes in the early years of movies, world famous Rodeo Drive, and discovering fantastic Mexican restaurants. We went shopping for lens filters for our cameras due to the smog we would find in Beijing and discovered that the clerks in the large department store had no idea where any other item was in that store! They were so spacey!

Our second encounter with how spacey people were in L.A. happened one evening when we lost our way and were sitting at a stoplight at about 11:00 at night. I rolled down the window and shouted to the lady in the next car, "Where is Highway 5?"

She answered, staring blankly straight ahead, "I have no idea where I am."

Soon we were in the sprawling place known as "LAX" (the L.A. Airport) where we eagerly introduced ourselves to members of our group. My friend said, "Oh, he's a pharmacist!  We'll probably be glad he's along!"

The flight was approximately 17 hours. That's unbelievable but true and of course we were in coach. I remember a very cruel, frightening movie shown on the plane of Japanese warlords cutting people up with their swords and I thought, Where am I going?  Whose idea was this?

Then a friendly steward on JAL approached us and said, "You already know a word of Japanese: 'Ohio.' That means hello."

At last we arrived and were so happy to walk around in the terminal. There I noticed lovely flowers in vases on the desks adding splashes of color in a steel gray and glass environment. A crowd of golfers was milling around.

Once we got our heavy bags we were off. I was struck by the orderliness of the movement of traffic and the number of police directing it and yet how quiet it seemed for such a large population.

We checked into our hotel—moderately priced for our tour—and examining our quarters I said to my friend, "Come and look at the bathroom!"

It was so clever. It was a molded unit of a bathroom that had been dropped into a space next to the bedroom. You had to step over the molded plastic threshold onto a molded plastic floor containing all the fixtures. I got the giggles in the shower because the Japanese are little people and the shower nozzle hit me about mid-chest instead of over my head.

Just as in the streets, there was no noise in the hotel. They are masters at insulation, apparently.

I discovered another weapon they use against noisiness with all those people: the restaurants I saw in the heart of Tokyo had outside patios with waterfalls, so there was no loud talking noise.

We couldn't wait for night to go to the Ginza or big shopping and restaurant area. We thought only the hostesses in a few fancy restaurants would be wearing kimonos, but much to our surprise more than half of the women we saw were clad in gorgeous kimonos. The rest were in conservative Western dress.

Soon we were off on a rather short flight to Beijing. It used to be "Peking" under British rule, but now it was a Communist city.

I got my first taste of a Communist country at the airport.

The Chinese ladies asked, "You mind we frisk you?"

I said, "Yes! I mind!"

But they smiled and patted me down anyway. Walking through the airport we were looking for the ladies' rooms and noticed that they had no door—just tattered dark red curtains that were about a foot higher than the floor.

We were all ushered onto a special bus that had a Chinese guide. This was to be true the whole time we were in China.

Oh, the ride into the countryside from the airport! Gazing out of the window at the rolling muddy fields punctuated by listless trees I saw an old, white haired woman with her hair in a bun laboriously pulling a cart—a cart with wooden wheels!

I exclaimed, "We've stepped back in time!"

Next I saw a peasant farmer relieving himself in a field.

The bus kept moving towards Beijing at a leisurely

pace. Traffic picked up—but what traffic! We saw truck after dilapidated truck piled high with rusty scraps of iron and withered brown leaves—just junk to us. This was our first lesson in how important everything is when you have such a tremendous, exploded population. Everything has value in the competitive race to survive!

Then came the bicycles! I didn't know there were these many bikes in the entire world! On every third or fourth corner was a bicycle repair shop. On the corners in between were enormous piles of winter cabbage, much higher than our heads. We soon realized that these were a diet mainstay in northern China. While we had seen some rice paddies in the countryside, we saw no selling of this grain on the sidewalks of Beijing.

We arrived at our hotel that looked fairly old and wasn't landscaped in the usual sense. It had many, many flowers in front, but they were all in flower pots. (Moveable scenery). We examined our "bare bones" hotel room with attached crude bath. We had read about this as having "western toilets" which we thought strange, but we soon learned that this crude plumbing was infinitely preferable to "eastern toilets" which usually translated into squatting over a stream!

Were we ever cold in that hotel room! We fiddled with the thermostat and had no luck so we decided to inquire at the desk. Meanwhile, my friend tried to put a call through to her boyfriend in Winchester, Virginia, to amaze him since she was pretty sure he had never gotten a call from China!

We found a thermos bottle of hot water in the room that was so hot it was bubbling! It was big and bulky and it was a hopeless task to pack but, oh, boy, did I want to bring that back! It was the best thermos I've ever seen. I tried and tried to cram it in, to no avail!

The next morning we eagerly attacked a manager type in the hall about not having heat in our room. He smiled and nodded and said, "November first! November first!" So that was the answer and since it was mid-October we had to wait!

Proceeding to our first breakfast in China we joined the 12 others at a big table in the dining room and were greeted by a waiter smiling and serving pejoe (beer), pears, and chocolate cake! I said that I guessed they had heard that Americans like chocolate cake! This was the beginning of being a tourist in China! I think our hosts really liked us and wanted to please.

We boarded our bus and met our Communist tour guides. The rules were clear. We were their charges and they were to show us how wonderful life was in China under Communist rule. We plunged into the world of heavy traffic from bicycles and crawling trucks, and over all smog. Many pedestrians wore surgical face masks!

We passed a doorway with an old lady vigorously sweeping her front stoop with a crudely made broom of twigs tied together at the top. A big cloud of dust rose on one side of her to descend on the other!

I asked our guides, Miss Lu and Daniel, a student, what made it so smoggy and Daniel explained that the wind blew sand from the Gobi Desert into Beijing where it would mix with fire and smoke from all the construction taking place in almost every block.

We studied the new buildings that, to us, looked like old buildings in America. We lurched to a stop and when it was time to go forward there seemed like a million people in front of us. The driver honked once, and when they didn't disperse, he just drove forward anyway. This was my first clue that with so many people, an individual life had very little value! Along these lines I asked our group if anyone had seen a hospital. (No one had). Had anyone heard a siren? (No one had). Beijing is an enormous city so this was very strange. While I was at it I asked if anyone had seen a dog? (No one had).

There were no groceries or drugstores as we knew

them so we were taken to what they did have for tourists who needed some items: "Friendship Stores". They were a real hodge-podge from aspirin to commie hats with the hammer and sickle on them.

We stopped on the street later to get ice cream at a little stand. They called it "bong bing" or something akin to that. Since there was never a drop of milk or cream or cheese to be had, I think this was our only dose of calcium for weeks!

I had big tears in my eyes when talking to the Chinese students.

These teenagers were all learning English and when we stood in Tiananmen Square they would approach us very politely and say, "Please we know that our English is not very good, but would you let us practice it on you?"

I would answer that indeed their English was perfect and that they sounded just like an American. They were so grateful that they would thank us profusely and give us a pin to wear of the flags of our two countries together. They were so sincere that it brought tears to my eyes! You can imagine how I cried several years later when they were being shot in Tienanmen Square, maybe some I had spoken to!

The square is very important to the Chinese

government and there were some government buildings in it, but mostly it was just huge like all the monuments we saw. It held many throngs of people— very few Americans and swarms of Chinese from all walks of life. They explained that their vacations are (or were then) spent in their country, at their magnificent monuments. There were lots of Mongolians in the square at that time, people who had come to the capital of China on their vacation, peasants who had never seen a city many of them.

We were mutually fascinated by them so we whipped out or Polaroid cameras to get quick photos and as we did so they encircled us, watching the film develop in silent fascination. Then as their picture appeared, they exclaimed, "Ohhhhh!" We felt we had to give it to one of them. They were so spellbound, so that necessitated taking a second picture each time!  One for us.

The "one child" policy was in full force, i.e. in order to receive government benefits, families were limited to just one child. (The government had noticed what we had remarked on:  too many people!). Families (almost all) wanted it to be a boy, to carry on the family name I guess. (And this was odd since there are so few surnames in China, like Lee and Wong). Anyway, as we traveled we noticed so many little boys and very few girls! The boys were adorable and often traveled with several family members who fawned over them. They wore the cutest knitted caps with big yarn pompoms on top. A sad rumor was that they had a bucket of water by the bed if the baby was a girl.

We noticed at the entrances to many giant monuments two lions on either side of the steps with one paw placed on top of the globe. Our guide explained the symbolism of China's ruling the earth.

As we clambered up the steps to these amazingly huge monuments, we noticed elaborately painted walls and ceilings inside—always the colors of gold and that orange-red that is "Chinese red." At one there was a wall outside surrounding it where, if you knelt and whispered a certain way, the whisper would travel all down that wall, come around its circle, and return to you, so we all tried that with varying degrees of success.

We loved the names of these monuments, names such as "The Temple of the Heavenly Peace."

One amazing monument was an actual boat made entirely of white marble that had served as a throne for an ancient Chinese princess. Of course, the boat didn't go anywhere but was on the edge of an idyllic lake surrounded by cherry blossoms.

This was all fabulous but nothing, to me, could

compare with The Forbidden City. You must go to China to see it because none of the amazing treasures it holds will ever go on tour. They are heavily guarded by Mandarins, Chinese people who still speak Mandarin and are garbed in the most gorgeous red and gold silks the world has ever seen! (Here the reader must make allowances for my somewhat incomplete or faulty recollections since more than 30 years have passed since I was in the Orient). I believe that here was the outside wall of elaborate mosaics forming a very colorful and enormous illustration of dragons and other mythical creatures.)

But I clearly remember what was inside! Here we were spellbound by the treasures we gazed upon, all safely behind glass. No touching! We saw jeweled ivory combs used by empresses and other jewels with which they were bedecked! There was so much of value on display in one place that words fail in describing them. We couldn't take pictures, alas! After we emerged into the sunlight along with some Chinese people on vacation, I wondered how these rag tag peasants could be so happy when they had so very little and many had to fight to survive. Our Chinese guide explained that they were very proud of their heritage and felt that they were part of all that. I couldn't imagine.

At last the big evening came!  Highly touted in our trip literature was 'The Peking Duck Banquet." We weren't sure just what we were eating in China!  (We never saw a dog or a cat.)

We walked in the cold, crisp air to the place where the restaurant was supposed to be, but it was just a dark building. There was a set of stairs so we climbed them. At the top was a large room, bare except for two large round tables with lovely floral centerpieces. But what caught our eyes were the napkins!  Like origami art, each one was folded beautifully and expertly into the shape of a bird or animal!  I have never seen such beautiful tables in my whole life!

To be honest the duckling was a bit overdone and dry, but the beautiful table settings made up for it. Our guide educated us to the very sad fact that our servers could never have afforded such a dinner as it would cost them a year's wages!  I felt awful about that!

We went to several lectures on business practices and anything that could be useful to Human Resources Directors while in Beijing. I recall one such meeting vividly as one could learn from it how the Chinese kept warm without furnaces. We were seated on low stools in a circle and served tea on low tables in front of us. Each mug containing hot tea had a lid that kept it warm. Further, when the Chinese professor next to me moved slightly, I could  see the cuff of his long underwear almost meeting his shoe.

As a matter of fact, once two of us were the last to get off the bus so Miss Lu leaned forward and whispered to us, "Do you have heat in your houses?"

We answered, "Yes, all of us, and we have air conditioning for hot days, too."

She stared sadly into space. The Communists tried to keep these things secret.

Daniel, our other Chinese guide, was a young student who wanted desperately to come to America. He so wanted to go to the University in Beijing, but it seemed impossible that he could. There were just too many good students!

We had our own Human Resources leader, a lovely gal who stressed that we were going to always have a voice in group activities and vote when there was a choice to be made. Her name was Shirley and she was very thin and frail and we worried about her.

On one trip out to see the catacombs and an historic tower which we climbed I saw some Chinese people emerge from a hole in the ground. Sadly, that was their home.

About the third day in Beijing, everyone but me

came down with a cold or a sore throat or both, so one of our friends approached me and asked if I really had brought bouillon cubes. I smiled and confirmed her question.

She said, "Barter! I have chocolate and we're both dying with colds and sore throats!"

I said, "How much chocolate?"

We had a lot of fun with that one!

We were very excited on the day we were to travel from Beijing out to see the Great Wall of China! One of the wonders of the world was almost in our grasp! We jumped onto the bus—no one was late this time—and headed out.

There was only one other group of American tourists that we ever saw back in 1984 and it was a nice seeming bunch from The University of Iowa. Often, we would arrive somewhere the nice seeming bunch were leaving. This illustrates how regulated tourism was. We were not allowed out of the sight of our Chinese guides.

We motored along the dusty Chinese roads to outlying villages, always gazing with interest at the sights. We didn't have any welcome snack or bathroom stops—there were no such conveniences! Imagine—no KFC's, McDonald's or 7-11's! Eventually, a bathroom stop was announced so we pulled over. We walked out and saw a few huts and fields and a stream. The stream was it! Some of us no longer had to "go"!

It was a long ride, but we finally saw the wall in the distance! As we approached we saw a lone camel in front of it whose owner offered rides. There was also a small gate you could enter and find on the other side a little souvenir shop so of course we descended on it, looking for a bathroom!

We climbed steps up to the wall and gazed down at the camel and then took in the miles of zigzag wall. We could see from that height the wall weaving its way across the mountains in both directions as far as we could see! It was punctuated by turrets—turrets with small holes which turned out to be windows so one could see the enemy approach. As we passed through a turret we were nearly crushed by many Chinese peasants and thought, "Why did everyone promoting this trip say that we didn't need any shots because China was so clean?" We were strongly wishing that we had had every shot they gave! We walked fairly far in both directions along with the crowd of Chinese on their holiday. I feel so fortunate to have seen it in spite of the conditions of the trip. They say it's the only thing on earth you can see from the moon but I don't know if that's true.

Later that day, it dawned on someone in our little group that we could subscribe to The China Daily newspaper (English edition) so we hurried to find out how to subscribe. The amazing fact hit us that because of the international date line, in China it was "the day before"! So when we got the paper from there it would be printed "the day before" which would make it current and correct when it arrived in the US on the next day's date there. That just blew the minds of all the business managers on the trip! They couldn't wrap their minds around that!

Suddenly we were faced with the choice of travel to our next destination, the ancient city of Xian. We could either get up on the morning and travel by bus to this destination where we would be housed in a "chicken coop" hotel, with no bathrooms or running water, or we could board the bus at 2 AM and receive box lunches and get there early and thereby get a regular hotel. Of course, most of us immediately voted for the latter. We staggered, half asleep, onto that bus and slumped down in our seats, using clothing for a pillow.

Ah! The things they didn't tell you! Off we careened with no headlights, bumping along half off the road. We asked why we had no lights on and the driver told us that we had to save energy with that big population. NOTHING IS WASTED! The problem was that since there were no street lights either, we ended up in farmers' fields several times and couldn't easily get out of the mud. Sometimes the men had to push!

Xian, the ancient capital, had several attractions, the most important of which was the excavation going on to uncover the ancient statues of soldiers buried there. We heard that a farmer turning over the dirt in his field had hit the head of a helmeted warrior, which caused him to dig and he found this amazing statue that was made of Terra cotta and was one of thousands buried with Quin Shi Huang, the first Emperor of China, in 210 B.C.! This was in 1974 and I believe the excavation is still continuing. No two are alike, either. I brought a very small statue home with me to always remind me. When we viewed this miraculous discovery, it was from bridges above the field where men worked night and day to uncover more soldiers.

But I'm a little ahead of myself. We'd checked into our hotel which was a nice one story sprawling affair, rather like a seedy, second rate motel on a state highway or byway in the States passed by big interstates, a "Bates Motel from Psycho," if you will.

I put my suitcase on a rickety chair and for some

strange reason started moving the faded pictures hanging on the walls. Bingo! There was a speaker set in the wall behind one. I pointed to it and we didn't say a word. We were very guarded in our remarks, never saying anything negative about China!

The other highlight of that trip to me was the most beautiful show imaginable that we were taken to that night. I have never seen anything to equal it. These very graceful dancers did scarf dances with brightly colored long silk scarves, weaving their dances around and through them, to beautiful music. It was like an other-worldly dream! My other recollection was that of being so cold in that seat that while I never wanted it to end, I was anxious to get warm somehow. I was interested to see that my friend who wasn't the slightest bit musical wasn't moved by this heavenly performance at all! Unbelievable!

When we returned to our Bates Motel we could tell that other hands had been rummaging through our suitcases! This whole schedule was set up so that they would have time to go through our possessions!

Xian was the city where the Silk Road began – the trade route that ended at the Mediterranean, linking China with the Roman Empire. This lasted from the second century B.C. to the end of the fourteenth century A.D. Silk was the major product of trade to travel this road. And what a fascinating sight it was to go into a silk factory there! Can you imagine watching hundreds of silk worms spinning silk? We expected factories like ours with assembly lines madly manufacturing widgets and here was a quiet place with silk spinning.

Xian also boasted amazing sculpted gardens that featured animals and birds of great size. For 3,000 years they have shaped and trimmed very impressive forms from the bushes, painstakingly keeping them perfect so that no twig was growing out to spoil the effect! There were huge pandas, perfect in every detail, as well as many other animals such as giant cows. We had never seen anything like it! Then, revisiting this place at night, they had come alive with many colors playing on them! It was a fairyland to walk through!

After a few days we were back on our bus headed for Hangzhou, a very picturesque city, capital of the Zheijang province. It was, at that time, a favorite honeymoon destination for the Japanese as it was beautiful and far less expensive than Japan was. I remember weeping willows bending gracefully next to West Lake and doctors seated under them with tables covered with white cloths and many pill boxes on them.

Evidently you would tell the doctors your ailment and they would supply you with pills. We walked pass this display and headed to a closer look at the lake.

West Lake was dotted with boats right out of the Arabian Nights. They were shaped basically like canoes except that both the bow and the stern rose about four feet into the air into a graceful point and in the center was a well-set tea table with pillows to sit on. It was easy to see why this was a sought-after honeymoon destination. It was very popular with the Japanese as it was a bargain compared to the high prices in their country and it was so picturesque and quiet there.

Our next discovery on another side of that lake area was the calligraphy taking place! About 20 Chinese people were kneeling or squatting over large poster-sized papers on which they were inking calligraphy. It was a beautiful art and I noticed calligraphy kits for sale from then on as we traveled through China. It was all a welcome change from the over populated, smoggy Beijing.

Our next stop was Shanghai and we were anxious to see it! We could appreciate why the trip was designed to go from north China to south China! Each town was an improvement over the last!

We rumbled into Shanghai staring at what was

before as—an old city on the banks of a river covered
with Chinese junks. The buildings looked dark and old
and were several stories high. Our hotel, The Shanghai
Mansions, was on the riverbank. I was fascinated by
the twisting, dark alleys and wondered if they led to
opium dens, the kind where you descend down steps
and lie on pillows and smoke long clay opium-filled
pipes. I really wanted to snoop around, but we were
always under the tutelage of guides furnished by this
Communist country.

We filed into the hotel lobby where a cheerful fellow
was behind the desk. Suddenly, on the shelf behind
him, I spotted a bottle of Four Roses!  I hadn't seen
anything remotely alcoholic in our whole Chinese visit
except for that weak pejoe!  (Beer). We were ecstatic
and felt that we had reached civilization again!  I never
drank a cheap brand of bourbon back home, but now
I prized it as if it were the most wonderful drink in the
world!

We were just in time for the entertainment: The Post
Office Band! We decided that the Chinese thought that
was a "hip" American name!  Soon we were dancing to
a bad, off rhythm American medley. I had somehow
acquired a dark haired, smooth Italian partner named
"Sergio." What joy it was to be dancing to American

music and drinking bourbon!  I felt like I'd just gotten out of jail!  So what if they played the notes in the wrong rhythm?  I stepped lively, whirled around and suddenly saw a big rat run across the floor quite near us!  I screamed and pointed and soon all the women on our trip were standing on the round wooden tables! We were still in China!

The next morning, I called out to my friend from across our bedroom where I had been staring out the window.

"Look!  Come here!" I shouted!  "What are they doing?"

On the sidewalks, bridges and boats below, the Chinese were doing a weird dance (or was it an exercise?) in slow motion, stretching their bodies into graceful movements, all doing different steps to the same dance. I had never seen anything like it. I found out that it was called "tai chi."  It looked like a great way to start the day—sort of like a cat stretching after waking up and before walking.

On this day we were slated to go to a commune of which the Chinese were very proud. I would have preferred to explore on my own, but we had to go places preordained that the Chinese wanted us to see!

Back on the bus we filed obediently. Soon we were

riding into rural outskirts and viewing miles and miles of winter cabbage in the fields. I had my picture taken in the field when we stopped. I was bending down, touching the cabbage with one hand and with a cigarette in the other. (This was the last year I smoked.)

Absolutely every Chinese man I saw smoked, though, and if they were taking a break they squatted in a circle and held that squat and talked and smoked a whole cigarette in that position! Their body type must be different from ours!

We continued on to the commune where our guide proudly led us to several buildings there. They had a "model kitchen" on display that made us feel very sad for them. For some reason 33 years later, I can still see it in my mind's eye. There was a lamp with red tassels in the corner and a small, coal burning stove.

The next building we entered had a kindergarten in it and the children (mostly boys!) were adorable. They had been trained to sing a song in English for their American visitors about how happy they were. It was a flawless performance. We clapped for them and would have enjoyed more time to mingle, but we were herded off.

That night we were treated to one of the highlights for tourists: the circus. Words are simply inadequate to describe the amazing balance that these mesomorph bodies have! They can all stand on their heads and do amazing tricks on little thin wires. We clapped until we had to leave. That was the best circus I've ever seen by a long shot! They did death-defying feats of balance with such ease!

The next day we were allowed to go shopping which was a real treat! I bought a cashmere sweater for my father and a brocade silk jacket for my mother, and, in one gorgeous store, I gazed and gazed at a blue and green cloisonné grandfather clock that I would have loved to have. I had to settle for pictures of it. The Chinese have mastered the art of cloisonné and we even saw them during this tour making designs with it and separating the little pieces with gold wire. Here I will also tell about their wonderful jade carving. Under running cold water they would patiently carve jade. I thought it must be very hard on your hands!

In the Friendship store, one of our group was very happy when he found a "Commie" hat and bought it as a souvenir.

For the first time since the start of our China trip, we were to board a plane to reach our final destination on that continent: Hong Kong!

We boarded a rather old-looking plane with propellers

instead of jet engines. When it took off there was a very loud mechanical popping sound so I turned to a man next to me and asked loudly, "What was that?"

He answered, "I don't know!"

I said, "You're supposed to calm the ladies down, not join in the fear!"

I reached into the pocket in back of the seat in front of me and extracted a vomit bag with Chinese letters on it. I tried to ready myself for a rough flight. Later I read that this was the least safe airline in the entire world!  I think it was CAAC or something like that. I was glad it was to be a short flight!

Once airborne, a smiling stewardess came down the aisle proudly bearing gifts for the passengers. I couldn't believe what they were: razors!  They were called "Rhino razors" and the package had a picture of a mean looking rhinoceros on it. Once again, they had part of the idea right, i.e., passing out something on the plane, but what it was made absolutely no sense—like serving us chocolate cake for breakfast.

Now suddenly we were circling. I have never seen a more beautiful sight than that harbor from the air!  It was unique to me in that the harbor was full of interesting boats, true, but the buildings around it climbed straight up like the sides of a bowl!  This gave it a 3-D quality unlike any harbor I had ever seen. And the buildings were very modern shiny steel and glass. It was the first city with a modern look and it was gorgeous!

Somehow the pilot landed safely and we practically ran into the airport. It was clean and modern inside and we reminded ourselves that Hong Kong was under British rule. There were some charming reminders that it was still in China, such as the rickshaws outside the airport but there were also cars, and what cars! They were Maserati, Rolls Royce limos, Mercedes limos, etc.! I have never seen that many expensive rides in one place. In fact, it was all I saw—no Fords or anything in a lower price range.

We had been told to do just two things in Hong Kong: eat and shop. And we were jumping up and down to taste both extravagances, but first we were to check into our hotel. No more "chicken coops" with questionable (or no) plumbing. We were happily ensconced in the Futurama, right next door to the pricey Mandarin. It was a very nice part of the city and it had a lovely bar. We were happy. We no longer had a Chinese guide with a set itinerary. We were totally free.

We couldn't help remarking how terrible this trip would have been if we had started in Hong Kong and worked our way to the cold, smoggy north! The temperature was wonderful – 75 degrees pretty constantly so we packed away our grungy jeans and brought out our shorts. We couldn't wait to ride the world-famous Star Ferry! For the sum of 25 cents you could sail away to another Hong Kong island. I remember the name "Kowloon." Oh, to sit back on one of the many seats on the ferry and gaze at the bright colored sails in sharp geometric cut patterns drift by! We would debark and swarm into huge outdoor malls—mostly open air with computers to buy everywhere (they were just catching on then), big glassy shop windows interspersed with Maxim's of Paris, and many other fine restaurants. It was like heaven after the deprivation we had been through. We were in Wonderland.

We wanted to have a fancy dinner to celebrate our return to sophistication and I had read about a sophisticated restaurant. So off we went on the Star Ferry at dusk. It was all a dream! We arrived at a lovely looking building, entered, and took an elevator down which opened into the restaurant. What a beautiful room with enormous crystal chandeliers, white linen tablecloths and waiters in tuxedos. We were shown to a table set for 12 places with a flute of champagne at each place.

We were ecstatic!  Strains of classical music wafted down on us. We assumed that the champagne was complimentary since we hadn't ordered it. (It was not!) It was such an enchanted evening, enjoyed so much more fully because of the contrast with what we had endured in Northern China! Several of the men in our group couldn't stop thanking me for knowing about this place!

The next day we explored, and, though on our own, we kept running into others from our group of 12 who were drawn to the same open air booths and shops. One of the big attractions was shopping for pearls. Hong Kong was famous for having a huge variety of them, so while we all had them, we wanted to look at what was there. This did nothing but confuse me to the point of not being able to buy any! The more I saw, the more I was dazzled and less able to discern. Besides who could trust these street venders?

I saw pearls with green casts, yellow casts, black casts, sparkling white, pink casts, you name it! All gleaming in the sunlight. Was one color more prized than another?  Who knew! Anyway, one lady in our group bought a beautiful pearl necklace, taking the risk regarding its true value. (We became friends and years later in the States she told me that she had had the necklace appraised and was very pleased with the result!  I should have been braver!)

We made another foray into the state-of-the art open malls—all glass and gleaming steel with escalators connecting the many floors. It was a banquet for the eyes after the dark smog preceding this city!

The British were still in control then which attributed greatly to the cleanliness, order and modern beauty. I never saw a scrap of trash the whole time. I do have one regret: that I never made it up Victoria Peak to see the amazing Hong Kong panorama. It's view of the harbor that rivals the one we saw from the air!

I couldn't leave this beautiful place called Hong Kong without promising myself I'd return. It was, and is, my favorite city!

# Japan

All too soon it was time to leave this paradise and head for Japan. We had a real "approach – avoidance" feeling about that destination due to all the rumors about how it was one of the most expensive places on earth and we were now at the bottom of our purses. In those days we carried Travelers' Cheques and credit cards weren't in use. Not only was it very expensive, but the Japanese were little in stature as a rule and the portions they served, consequently, were small.

After we landed in Tokyo, we were ushered into a restaurant for dinner. Interestingly, the head waiter bowed deeply. We learned that the more important a person was, the deeper was the bow. We deducted that we were semi-important!  I believe we had sushi and I can't think what else.

The next day we were slated to hear a lecture at a university in the Tokyo area. We were amazed to see all of the modern motorbikes in the parking lot there in stark contrast to the bicycles of Beijing. We were ushered into an attractive clutter free classroom with computers everywhere!  This was very advanced at that time.

Later in the day we went to a very important place—the Department of Labor where we were permitted to ask questions. We sat at a large U-shaped table along with the neatly dressed Chinese officials, each in dark suit fielding questions thrown by our Human Resources crew—questions regarding Japanese practices in the workplace. I took notes as always. Travel fatigue was beginning to overtake me, but just then the table in front of me shook and then my chair moved back and forth as well! My mind tried to explain this to my shaking body. It said, "We must be over a train station."

One of the officials smiled and said one word "earthquake," which he pronounced "earthcake."

Wow! Who knew! But they are a regular occurrence in Japan!

Soon it was time for lunch so I bid "Adieu" to our hosts and a group of us headed for a pizza joint in order to ingest homey food again. I don't remember a thing about lunch except a three-year-old little Japanese child crying uncontrolled – sobbing without cessation because he had spilled a little pizza sauce on his white shirt! I said, "They must be born neat!".

Emerging into the sunshine, I was struck again by the neat, uniformed look of the little boys—all of their socks pulled up to just below the knee cap, all the shiny, black, straight hair cuts were identical ending just above the eyebrows, all the navy blazers identical except for different colored school crests on the pocket. My friends discussed how this uniformity affected the individuals and their careers, subservient to their companies. We were also struck by the small size of their apartments and the great size of the population.

Some of us wanted to see their department stores so we embarked upon a voyage of discovery. Once again, I was the only one to notice another cultural difference. Outside the big glass entrance doors stood a rectangular box about 4 feet tall filled with small square spaces slightly larger than an ice cube. Umbrella handles protruded from about half of them. You were to insert your wet umbrella in to a small square space and lock it in with a key you then carried with you. No such thing allowed as a messy, wet dripping umbrella on the clean floor inside!

That night we headed for the Ginza, the big shopping and eating district. We were amazed at all the beautiful Kimonos we saw there. We noticed that entire menus, being in front of the restaurants had pictures of the food so that we foreigners could just point to what we wanted. We saw many beautiful articles of apparel for sale but mostly felt we needed to save money but window shopping was lovely.

We had befriended a fun couple on our trip so we decided to have a "nightcap" with them and found an inviting lounge so I treated myself to two liqueurs and left for my hotel room. I reached for the doorknob and missed—it seemed to move further away! I thought, "Those little drinks must have been stronger than I thought! Woo!" The next day everyone was talking about the earthquake last night. Whew! What a relief.

Japan experiences these tremors all the time. It's made up of volcanic islands with a mind of their own! My last encounter with an earthquake occurred at a really bad time—when I was crossing a bridge spanning over a busy street. I was in the middle of the bridge when I had to hold onto the side. That was a severe tremor too!

One day we took off again and got to see the ancient capital of Kyoto which was capital of Japan for 1,000 years plus. The main attraction was a palace famous for its creaking boards. The legend was that the Emperor had enemies who might try to sneak up and kill him so he had a creaking board installed. Anytime someone stepped on it, it would loudly squeak.

We saw a beautiful sight and learned that the components of a Japanese garden were wood, stone and water. There was a very picturesque scene before us of a wooden house up high with a cascading waterfall under it, falling over grey stones. Cherry blossoms surrounded the house.

Japan doesn't have the bright orange reds and golds of China; rather it features the serene calmness of browns and greys and that's true of their palaces.

The Imperial Palace in Tokyo once housed Hirohito and his family. It is a huge complex with separate buildings for living and for ruling. We parked our bus in the huge lot there but weren't allowed to get very near.

Some human-interest stories remind me of the Disney attraction, "It's a small world after all!"

I saw a grandmother in a hotel lobby proudly wearing a Mickey Mouse hat with big round ears, talking to her granddaughter. They had just returned from a visit to Tokyo's Disney World. I remember the happiness on their faces.

The second scene is that of a very proud father taking pictures of his debutante daughter on a pedestal in a hotel, her creamy satin dress swirling in front of her. His face was truly beaming.

One of our most interesting experiences was riding the ultra-high-speed Bullet Train from Tokyo to Kyoto. We were told that the doors were timed to stay open for a very short time, so we stationed the men in front of us with our bags, purses, etc., which they threw on, jumping on afterwards and then putting us on! The world truly rushed by in a big blur, but the ride was so smooth!

We went to our hotel room to change clothes in preparation for the highly touted "Farewell Banquet." I was wearing my blue suede suit that was made for me "overnight!" from measurements taken that day and delivered to my room. Waiters bowed a little lower than usual as our party entered. We were dying of anticipation. There was a huge round loaf of bread on a cart with wheels that was brought to us and if it hadn't been for that we would have starved to death! Their portions of our dinners were very small and there were no seconds. We were resourceful people, so we gathered after the meal and decided to go to one of the nearby shopping centers and go in every restaurant there and have a dessert in each and just spend the rest of the Japanese money. We called it "The Night of Ten Thousand Desserts." We were grinning from ear to ear!

One of the delights Japan offered was Kentucky Fried Chicken. We were so excited to get some American food again and I was delighted to meet another cultural difference head-on. There was a giant poster of Colonel

Saunders, Japanese style, with slanted eyes and under a cherry tree.

The flight back to LA the next day was quite rough due to a strong tail wind, but we arrived an hour earlier than the flight over!

All I remember about LA on the return trip was going in a big noisy American (!) restaurant with TV's overhead blaring out football games. We felt like space travelers who had returned to earth with a crash! The blinding, deafening, familiar world was in front of us. I said, "It's Monday Night Football! Remember Monday Night Football?"

The waiter brought us huge menus and we ordered so many dishes we were starved for from steak to shrimp to prime ribs. The water gasped and said, "You can't eat all that!"

I said, "You don't understand! We've been to China and Japan. We're starved for this food! We CAN eat it!

Landing in Dulles, I was terrified to see what short-term parking had cost me, but between us, we scraped up the money!

# Who Am I?

I really never liked my surname and was happy to get married and change it. I was tired of people making fun of it in the form of tired jokes about my galloping somewhere. You couldn't poke fun at my new surname, "Armstrong," unless you really had nothing to do.

After I had been selling real estate for about twenty-five years, which really DID feel like a quarter century, I was walking down my sidewalk when my cell phone rang. The man's voice on the other end asked, "Is this Judith Gallup Armstrong?"

I was so startled to hear my whole name that I couldn't answer for a minute. I finally said, "Yes."

"This is Roger Gallup," the voice continued.

I was dumbfounded. The only Roger Gallup I had ever known about was the son of one of Dad's brothers and I had heard that he was dead.

"Who?" I asked helplessly.

"I am the son of your grandfather Gallup," the man continued.

Now I sat down on the edge of a large flower box beside my front door.

The man told me that after my paternal grandparents divorced, my grandfather remarried and had two children, a boy and a girl, and he was the boy. He was calling from California, where he lived, and I thought about all the times I had been to San Francisco and how sorry I was that I didn't know about him then!

Thus began a wonderful correspondence while I tried to figure out our relationship. Was he my step-uncle? Thanks to the internet, he was able to send me pictures of my grandfather Gallup so I could see what he looked like. I was only a year old when my grandparents divorced, so I had no idea of his appearance other than a black & white photo that showed him at a distance.

Step-Uncle Roger also sent me family pictures with his new family, plus Grandfather Gallup's World War One draft card and other memorabilia. What a delightful revelation!

Step-Uncle Roger was in the process of writing a book about my grandfather and appreciated family photos I sent of his children by his first wife, my Nana Gallup. It was such fun to have someone to reminisce with regarding the family that I knew growing up. It was delightful to have someone to laugh with about Uncle Paul, Dad's brother, because we both knew him well. We got in lengthy discussions about how Paul would show up with no notice, just appearing on the doorstep with his current fiancée. Paul was so funny that I clearly remember Mother laughing heartily!

This connection to my past, Uncle Roger, was such a wonderful, warm and welcome surprise, and to learn that he and his five sons all exhibit a mixture of the same talents my father had (art, music and selling) was incredible. It was fun to see these talents flowing through the family!

Not long after this miracle appeared unbidden in my life a second one occurred! I walked into my real estate office one day and the secretary greeted me with:

"Your cousin from Hawaii called."

I was floored! What cousin in Hawaii, I wondered. I really thought it was a mistake. With trembling fingers, I called the number. A woman answered and informed me right away that she was the wife of one of my Uncle Paul's children! She said that she worked with computers in the credit bureau there and was familiar with the research done by the Mormons on family trees, so she decided to "give her husband his family for his birthday."

She told me I was able to be traced through the "officiant" at my father's funeral in Indianapolis. We had a lively conversation during which I told her that I was planning to attend a real estate meeting in Oahu for Certified Residential Specialists. She invited me to join her and her husband afterwards on the big island of Hawaii. I quickly acquiesced and wished strongly that my parents were still alive, so I could share all this news, plus the discovery of "Step-Uncle" Roger!

I loved the convention hotel in Oahu, with its wall-less check-in desk. I thought that they must lock up things of value in a little room behind the check-in counter because I could see out in every direction – all the way to the sandy beach and the waves beyond! The Hilton actually had a campus with small hotel buildings scattered about and a lovely row of exclusive shops, all blending in with the architecture. There was a row of torches leading down a walkway to the beach – torches that were lit each dusk with accompanying Hawaiian music.

After check-in, I reached a corner with palm trees swaying and came upon an islander sitting on a low wall, strumming his ukulele and signing. I caught him in the act of being happy, and who wouldn't be in the persistent 73-degree weather?

That night, I attended my first authentic luau with pig on a spit and all the trimmings. I met the others who flew to this meeting and knew one other member who was from Richmond. The next day, I sat across from the biggest diamond ring I've ever seen in my life! People up and down the lunch table were nudging each other, that's how huge it was. Some people thought they should move to the island and sell real estate because it must reward you with enormous commissions!

Finally, a man seated near me spoke to its wearer saying, "Excuse me, but could you tell me how many carats that ring has?"

"Nine," she answered.

He stated that business here must be very good!

"Oh, no," she said, "That's a gift from my husband." She added that he owned a pineapple plantation.

I loved swimming there the next day and admiring Diamond Head close by. The water was clear and sparkling and very calm. I floated and watched the puffy clouds and seagulls.

I noticed a great number of Japanese men on vacation, each sporting a camera as an accessory around the neck. This caused me to coin a new phrase, "Naked as a Japanese man without a camera."

I attended several real estate meetings, not cheerfully because the beaches were beckoning to me. But I found the speakers to be entertaining and instructive, so I was glad to learn some useful pointers.

The days hurried by as they always do when you don't want them to, and soon I was in the airport awaiting the plane to the Big Island where my cousin and his wife were anxious to meet me. I was directed to a row of benches stretched out beneath palm trees and I thought how divine it was to wait for a plane in such surroundings! Of course, the flight was quite short, as the puddle-jumper went down almost before it went up!

I spotted the rental car desk and got in line. I stood there arguing with myself. Should I be smart and get a small car and save money, or go for a shiny convertible? After all, how long was the wait going to be for another trip to Hawaii? By the time I was next in line, my mind was made up. I was going to ask for a convertible!

Screwing up my courage to the sticking place, I approached the big, double-chinned, wavy-haired brunette behind the counter. I mumbled that I had decided to rent a convertible.

Her eyes flashed so that now her resemblance to Roseanne Barr was complete! She looked at me scornfully and shouted, "In your dreams!"

This took me by complete surprise. Finally, I asked softly, "Does that mean you don't have any?"

She spat out that if a visitor wanted a convertible they had to request it months in advance! I meekly sputtered away in a boring gray sedan – I don't remember what kind.

I pulled up in front of a warehouse where I was to meet Gail, my cousin's wife, who had arranged this whole reunion. She jumped out of her car and introduced herself and invited me to grocery shop with her. We entered this cavernous structure with rows upon rows of groceries which had to be imported in large quantities to this island. After she checked out some groceries, I followed behind her in my car to their house, which was inland on the edge of a sugar cane field. The house rose above the cane and was inviting with a Swiss chalet appearance.

Gail's parents lived next door and had been invited for dinner and to meet me. At last I saw my cousin, Shelley, who was a big, strong rather beefy man. He didn't look at all like the little blond, blue-eyed chubby legged toddler I remembered from my baby-sitting days. He certainly knew how to barbecue, though! We sat on the deck and watched the setting sun paint the scenery with a broad orange brush – what a memorable evening!

My quarters were in a garage apartment, which had been constructed by my cousin and consisted of a large bedroom and bathroom with shower.

Since both of my hosts were working, I made my way to Kona in my boring gray sedan and signed up for a whale-watching boat-trip. It was guaranteed that we would see whales. I asked the captain how he could be so certain. He smiled and said, "It's mating season!"

Boy was he right! There were whales spouting, rolling and diving all over the place!

I enjoyed exploring Kona. Since it's famous for its coffee, I entered a coffee shop to enjoy a cup. The manager said that they were closing. I couldn't imagine why, so he explained that since the advent of the internet, they could fill so many orders and they didn't need to have stores anymore. That was sad news to Kona tourists!


I discovered a hotel with a very nice beach, a bar covered with a thatched roof and surrounded by palms, and a guitarist who sat on a stool and played. This met all of my requirements, so I spent a lot of time there. No one ever discovered that I wasn't staying at that hotel!

One large family group spread out on the towels said that they worked hard all year and took no vacations but saved up for their annual trip from California to this hotel on the Big Island. I could certainly understand why!

One day, my cousin and his wife took me snorkeling and it was so interesting! On the way, I saw some interesting sights – a snow-capped mountain where you could ski all year, a volcano that was dormant, so we walked up close, and beaches of different colored pebbly sand, depending on what kind of rock was there. I had never seen a green beach or a black beach before! We snorkeled at the black beach location, which was a lot of fun! I saw brightly colored fish swimming in and out of the coral. Most of them, like the Blue Stripe Snapper and the Longnose Butterfly Fish, were predominantly a vibrant yellow. The effervescence of the yellow against the black sand was startling and exquisite.

Another day, I decided to traverse the island in my boring gray sedan and see Hilo on the distant side. When I was young, I learned the song, "The Hilo Hattie Hop." The road was very curvy and went through a lot of jungle scenery punctuated by crashing waterfalls within nearly every hairpin turn. It took my breath away!

At last, I started seeing hotels on the outskirts and I began to drive through the little town. There was a big museum that caught my eye, so I parked the boring car and entered. Inside, the gallery contained floor to ceiling photos that horrifically depicted people desperately trying to run from the huge, all-engulfing waves of a tsunami. What a terrible sight! I walked through, overcome by the faces of fear on every wall.

After all that, I found a nice, calm, colorful museum displaying fabrics and art objects.

That night, my cousins and I went to dinner at a very lovely restaurant back in the Kona area – all open air and serving wonderful seafood.

I retired to my garage apartment, got into bed, and saw a rat as big as a fox terrier scurry across the floor! I screamed bloody murder and reached down for my shoe which I hurled at the rat (and missed!).

I was badly shaken, so I grabbed a robe and scrambled out the door and across the back yard to the main house. I barged in the back door and when Shelley appeared, I told him about the rat. He responded that I must be mistaken. I assured him that I wasn't and said I would gladly sleep on the couch, which I did.

After that incident, things became a bit strained between us. I spent the last day at the beach as usual and came back in time for dinner, but there seemed to be no preparations being made. I asked if we were going out to eat but they replied that they had been someplace on the island and decided to eat early dinner there. End of sentence. I then said, "Well, I guess I'll find a restaurant then." I asked around and found one not far away. I sat eating my last meal on the Big Island alone and reading and contemplating my visit. It was one of those times when I wished my mother had been alive.

I returned the gray sedan and flew back to Oahu the next morning. I was met at the airport by Uncle Paul's daughter. We'd arranged this meeting while I was on the Big Island. I had not laid eyes on Linda since she was in her crib! She certainly had grown! She was the only Gallup I knew with brown eyes, so I called her "my brown-eyed cousin." My grandmother Gallup had brown eyes but she had married into the blonde, blue-eyed Gallup family. Anyway, we hit it off right away and were delighted to meet each other. She had the family sense of humor! She told me how much she loved it there and wanted to stay and never go back stateside. She had a secretarial job and a live-in boyfriend. They had a nice townhouse with a patio overlooking a beautiful waterfall. She loved everything about it. We had dinner there, enjoying the scenery and the cool air.

The time passed all too quickly and Linda and her boyfriend drove me to the airport.

My head was spinning on the flight to California with all of these amazing experiences. The beauty of the Hawaiian Islands has stayed with me always! Happily, I have been blessed to return to the Hawaiian Islands since that time – to Maui!

# Maui

Each Island has its own allure. The first time I ever visited Maui, I invited a very good friend who told me she would love to come as it was on her list.

I was so fortunate because I had become an "owner" with Westin, and at that time I could enjoy a week in their lovely hotel there during the fall or early winter period. We chose late October for our trip and flew out together from Dulles to Los Angeles and then to Maui. It's a really long haul from the East Coast, but worth every mile!

During the interminable flight west, I pulled out the hotel information to show to Gloria. After scanning it, she asked where we were staying the first night.

Oh no! What a shock! I hadn't counted right, and we were arriving a day BEFORE our hotel reservations began! I was in a panic.

Immediately after landing in L.A., I went right to the phone and made some frantic calls. I recommended myself I don't know how many times, but I finally got a two-bedroom condo on the grounds of some hotel in Maui. The good fortune gods were smiling broadly because we loved it! It didn't have water views, but it did feature a short walk to the beach where everything wonderful awaited. We really liked it as it was a small, understated place with friendly people.

Soon we were off again in a taxi with our luggage for the Westin Kaanapali, where I had a free vacation for a week. What a gorgeous hotel! The drive was lined with palms gently bobbing and swaying in the breeze. There were no walls, just open space with ocean and garden views!

We found our second floor, two-bedroom suite and explored it happily, then went out to sit on the balcony facing the courtyard with ocean views. At that very moment, we heard strains of ukuleles and some Hawaiian dancers magically appeared right in front of us and danced the hula!

Gloria is quite the organizer and soon she had us signed up for a luau and a wonderful show about Hawaii. I relaxed and enjoyed these events. We strolled over to the beach where several pigs were turning on a spit over fire. Inviting picnic tables were groaning under the weight of pineapples, strawberries, and all sorts of colorful treats. Brilliantly colored tropical flowers were scattered across the tables. Ukuleles were strummed and everyone was smiling broadly. The experience was so vibrant and redolent with scents and sounds that the memory will remain etched in my mind forever.

A free bus ran us into Lahaina, the town that was just a few miles away, so we decided to see what it had to offer. I was quite surprised to enter one of many art galleries and behold several genuine Picassos which could be bought! I thought that I was obviously not one of their regular clientele! I had a lovely time looking, though! For lunch we had to go to the famous "Cheeseburger in Paradise" and sing the song. The restaurant had a second floor with marvelous views.

After lunch, we walked around the area. There was one jeweler who really stood out, so we went in to visit. Since I like to buy a ring at almost every place I travel, I decided to look at the pearls, since Hawaii has so many due to the pearl diving industry. I settled on a large one surrounded by very small diamond chips. I fell in love with it and just had to have it!

We had heard much about "The Road to Hana", which was supposed to be one of the most beautiful places on earth and chosen by Lindbergh as his burial site. It runs along the back side of Maui and is acclaimed as the "longest scenic route in the world." There has never even been such a terrifying curving road up in the air with no shoulders, just a thin piece of spaghetti with hairpin curve after hairpin curve! That's about as scared as I've ever been, seated in a rickety white van with no way to tell if anyone was coming in the opposite direction!

We did make some memorable stops and got out to walk around. I saw beautiful waterfalls, some very tiny villages, a rest room with a billfold someone had left by the sink – probably someone too scared to think straight! – and, yes, Lindbergh's grave. His grave was just a simple stone marking the spot where he planned to lie and gaze at the sky and sea forever.

The trip took almost all day and we were glad to get back into relaxed vacation mode at the end of the day.

The following day was October 31, Halloween, which hadn't been in our thoughts at all until some teen-aged boys yelled across the street at us saying, "Well, where's your costume?"

They almost sounded angry!

"We forgot the date," we said.

Then I added, "All we have are Hawaiian shirts and leis anyway, so that wouldn't be a costume here in Maui!"

They shook their heads and moved on.

What a wonderful job they do with that holiday in the islands! I wonder if it has to do with voodoo?

Every single person was in costume. Some were so funny we laughed until we cried! We sat outside having cocktails at a restaurant near our hotel and were waited on by the Tin Woodman and the Scarecrow from "The Wizard of Oz." The scenery was filled with zombies, exotic birds and everything you could think of. Some were so humorous that our sides ached from laughing. We marveled at the original ideas and the money spent on elaborate costumes!

We had made dinner reservations in Lahaina, so off we went in the van loaded with costumed people!

As we started to go into the restaurant, we stopped to watch the official annual parade march by and there was a loud band playing. In front were two pilots appearing drunk with their hats and ties askew. One was asking what time the plane was to take off and the other said he had no idea! I am so glad we stumbled into such a happy time!

On the way back from this delightful trip, we stumbled upon a beautiful jazz brunch in Lahaina with gorgeous views of the Pacific – the perfect end to our trip! The jazz was straight from New Orleans and the seafood dishes were superb, and the sparkling blue waters of the Pacific were paradise!

Quite recently, I returned to Maui and had a

marvelous, though entirely different time. I travelled there with my daughter, Deb, and her partner.

In one of those amazing coincidences, I met some nice people in the swimming pool who, like I, were originally from Omaha. It was pleasant to renew old memories. These people now had moved to California and one man was the manager for a famous television political pundit. Since this star was of the opposite political persuasion, we had some interesting conversations!

We three took a lovely boat trip out from the island at sunset and invited a nice lady who had a baby-sitting job part-time with a vacationing family from Maine. As we got to know her we discovered that she and Barbara Bush walked their dogs together at Kennebunkport. There was another star association!

I spent time exploring another chic hotel and its lovely restaurants and shops, and of course, I was always near or in the water!

# The Russian Enigma

One day I noticed an article about an upcoming trip to Russia in a Mary Baldwin College magazine, and I thought "Wow! That's on my list! I think I'll go!" I never thought about asking anyone to go with me. Why, I'd have MBC alumnae and students as well as a faculty member along with me! What fun!

The faculty member who led the trip had lived there and spoke fluent Russian, which made it ideal for making many complicated arrangements, getting us tickets to events at regular prices rather than inflated prices for the tourists, etc.

I soon learned why prices were more affordable for the group of students who made up a large percentage of our group: the hotels were quite distant from the important places in the heart of towns, or they were conveniently located, but very antiquated and not in the least bit luxurious!

Our first stop was Moscow, which is a city I'll never forget! My first impression while riding in from the airport was row upon row of dismal gray buildings that were apartments. There was almost no green space –

neither grass nor flowers. A line with laundry hanging forlornly on it occasionally appeared to break up the gray monotony.

We arrived at our hotel, which was just steps away from Red Square. I was delighted to be so close! When we alighted from the bus, we were instructed to go in one door only, as a lot of the hotel was undergoing renovations. We learned that in order to enter our rooms, we went in one door, but for the cafeteria, we had to go out that door and walk around the end of the old structure and enter another door, climb inside steps and be sure to remember our breakfast ticket. All this effort in the cold climate was rewarded by an array of mostly root vegetables – vegetables that grow underground, such as beets (think borscht!), potatoes and carrots. We shrugged and accepted this as a very peculiar breakfast!

Shortly after our first breakfast, we assembled in the hotel room of our group leader, "Vladdy," who gave us a very interesting dissertation on this strange new land, or "Why They Behave Like Russians." First, he talked about Russian geography and explained that Moscow is very far from the ocean, and thus doesn't benefit from its moisture. Because of this it is indeed a hostile environment for fruits and many vegetables, so their staple food is any form of root vegetable such as we had already dined upon.

We were anxious to explore, so we descended on Red Square. St. Basil's Cathedral presided majestically over the end of it, very near our hotel. It was awe-inspiring up close, with its beautiful gold dome and bright blues and shining stars! Its spires are world famous. Today it is a museum.

From there we walked the length of the square which I had pictured as endlessly enormous from the parade of tanks I had seen on TV, rolling by reviewing stands full of stern faced Russian military officials. It was very surprising that it wasn't huge at all – about the length of a few blocks. On the right was the well-known Gum department store, which they pronounce "Goom" rather than "Gum." On the left there were steps leading underground to the heavily guarded Lenin's tomb. Seeing it is a very big deal and although our group had gained admittance, I had a camera in my hand, so the guards denied me the privilege of admittance. I offered to let them hold the camera while I toured, but they refused so I never did get to see Lenin's tomb! (See previous comment, "Why they behave like Russians?" Who can explain these things?)

On a lighter note, since I couldn't see Lenin's

tomb, I decided to sashay into Gum. I'd heard that it was a mecca for Russian shoppers. I expected a large department store, but found instead an attractive glass-roofed array of chic shops such as you would expect in any world capital. The high glass ceiling was lovely with some colored glass fragments. I wandered past all the famous boutiques until I heard a "drip, drip, splash!" sound and beheld a bucket in front of one of the counters into which drops of water were falling, right past the diamond and sapphire necklace on the counter.

I walked out smiling to myself, watching the parade of Russians passing by. There were very old men, all gnarled and bent, with dark robes and carved walking sticks and old women, heavy-set and wrinkled, wearing long black dresses and wrapped in shawls. They were the "babushkas", which is Russian for "grandmother."

All of these old people appeared to be looking down and frowning. I felt a hopelessness emanating from those gnarled frames. The youth who strolled along, also clad in dark colors for the most part, seemed cheerful and purposeful, which was a good sign and lifted my spirits.

At the far end of Red Square arose a spanking new McDonald's, of all things! I could hardly believe my eyes. The funniest thing about it was that the teenagers really flocked to it, since it was American in concept. They "hung out" with friends enjoying fries and burgers late and night, thinking that was what American teens do!

It was so cold in Russia that I needed to buy a heavy sweatshirt to go under my lined raincoat. Thankfully I discovered a Hard Rock Café shop on one of the side streets. I bought a sweatshirt there that said "Moscow" across the front. It was way too expensive, but the price was quickly forgotten as I snuggled into it.

One morning, we stood in snow flurries waiting outside the gate to an exhibition of the famous Faberge eggs. The time dragged, but we stood our ground. At last, the magic time arrived, and the guard slammed the gate shut and said, "No more showings!" (See, again, the former comment, "Why they behave like Russians!")

The next day was exciting as we were to be allowed into the Kremlin! How thrilling! We walked the length of Red Square, passed McDonalds, turned and watched the soldiers standing at attention by the tomb of the Unknown Soldier, and we were admitted through the massive gates onto the cobblestones of the Kremlin! As we walked past big, gray buildings, we came upon an

English-speaking tourist in front of them who shouted to us: "Whatever you do, don't take a picture of this building! I did and they confiscated my camera! The guards are making me wait here!"

We felt so sorry for him, but there was nothing we could do. As we stood across the street from him, a long black limousine rolled by. Looking in, I saw Putin in the back seat. Needless to say, he wasn't smiling!

After this adventure, we walked with some trepidation into a beautiful Russian stone church nearby. I have never seen such beautiful mosaics in my life. They were so large and intricate with many tiny pieces forming the figures of saints who stretched from floor to ceiling!

Our visual banquet was enhanced by an auditory one, for the most beautiful men's voices sang out the entire time, but the choir was invisible! I have no idea where they were. Instead of one altar, there were many altars scattered about, with people kneeling at all of them. It was a very moving religious experience.

Late the next afternoon, we assembled at the train station to travel overnight to St. Petersburg. We boarded and separated into small roomettes. When I entered my roomette, I cried out that there was trash on my bed! An official pushed his way in and explained that it was actually an old, brown wrinkled sack which contained supper for me. It was just another uniquely Russian gustatory experience. I had to sleep in my clothes and of course there was no opportunity for baths!

I was delighted that the personnel at the hotel in St. Petersburg spoke English, but surprised that they asked for our passports. They said they would be kept safe behind the desk with them. I underwent separation anxiety as I surrendered mine.

It was easy to see why this beautiful Russian city was named as Russian's capital at one time. St. Peter the Great declared it to be in 1712. In 1918, Lenin moved the capital back to Moscow. The Neva river flows gently through St. Petersburg, and we crossed it on bridges quite often as well as taking cruises on it.

Soon after our arrival, we were touring Peterhof, the palace of Peter the Great. It is so memorable, with many fountains and outdoor staircases descending next to them. Statues enhance the many gardens. During World War Two, they buried the statues, so they wouldn't be taken. Peter the Great was cool and decided to have a log cabin built for his relaxation instead of always being in a formal palace. He also had a great sense of humor. He had hidden sprinklers installed all over an outside patio so that people would get squirted when they walked on it!

We also learned all about Rasputin and the hold he had over the queen, wife of Tsar Nicholas II, who thought he could cure her son. We got to tour the house where Rasputin finally met his end.

My favorite tour was, of course, The Hermitage, the magnificent castle of Katherine the Great. I was always fascinated by her when I studied world history. The intelligence and love the of the arts she possessed was remarkable and I thought she imitated the French court of the time. I found out that she surpassed the French Court! If Fontainebleau had several fountains, she would have many more! She imported courtiers to teach her courtiers French. The French were her models, but she outdid them at every turn. She played card games with her ladies-in-waiting using diamonds and other precious jewels instead of money. Meanwhile, the peasants were starving on the streets. She also had windows installed all over the palace – a fairly new invention at the time and very expensive!

The most impressive room is the Amber Room – a chamber decorated in amber panels backed with gold leaf mirrors. Some considered it the "Eighth Wonder of the World." It contains over 13,000 pounds of amber. During World War Two the amber was looted by the Nazis. Its current whereabouts are a mystery, but the room has been reconstructed.

I saw room after room of Picassos as well as every famous artist in the world! There were rooms of sculptures, tapestries and objects resplendent with jewels – it was mind-boggling! I discovered that in the time of Katherine's reign, art was the sign of wealth, so the more you had, the more powerful a monarch you were considered.

I pranced up to the desk on the first floor and asked for a book about every artifact and painting in The Hermitage. The man behind the desk stared at me coldly. At length he said, "If you stood in front of every object of art of five minutes, it would take you ten and a half years to see it all. No, we couldn't possibly put it all in one book."

The next day, our group split up and went exploring – mostly walking around. One gentleman and his brother-in-law went out and were attacked by a gang of Russian youths who surrounded them and took their billfolds and cameras. The gentleman was far more upset about the theft of his camera than his billfold. He had pictures of the old babushka who told him all about World War Two and how much she admired Stalin. It had really fascinated him. He borrowed a second camera, and that was also stolen by Russian youth!

After this, Vladdy met with us and said that Russia was a Third World country and therefore many youths had no job and preyed on tourists, knowing where they would be. There were also Gypsies to beware of, so it wasn't safe to go out alone. We were henceforth go out in groups of at least four people, and we had to sign out at the front desk of the hotel.

Just after this, we saw the front page of a Russian newspaper in which there was a large picture of a band of Gypsies completely surrounding someone and stripping them bare so that nothing could be hidden from them! I now understood why we left our passports at the front desk!

There were some cute Russian college-aged kids who knew some of the people in our group, so they showed us around at night. I was so glad to be with them. The first night we went to a nice Indian restaurant. The food was delicious and a welcome change from Russian root vegetables!

The next night we had an amazing time! We went to a restaurant called "Stalin's Mating Call"! I bought place mats as souvenirs to prove that was the actual name of the place! We entered and were greeted by a matronly woman who led us to a long table in a candle-lit room. I kept sensing that there were several sinister looking people who looked exactly like spies. Up high in all four corners was a small TV set with scenes of huge tanks rolling along in World War Two. As we watched, the scenes changed to steamy love scenes. I can't remember what I ate, but I could draw a picture of that room!

When we were done with dinner, we walked out, but instead of getting a cab we followed our Russian student guides around the corner to a grey cement two-story building with steps up to the door. There were no windows or signs – nothing! Pulling the heavy door open, we were greeted by singing and toasting as we watched Russian youths gaily piling their beer mugs on top of each other as they sat on high stools at round metal tables! They sang and chanted cheers and swigged their beers! There was a glass wall behind them, revealing huge vats of the golden brew and there was a big bar running down the middle of the room. To my eyes, it was so strange to not have a sign advertising the place!

We strolled to the Bolshoi Ballet building one afternoon and entered and enormous gift shop. The gifts and souvenirs formed an impressive display.

The night we were going to see the opera "Carmen"

with Russian words was unforgettable! We set out in slacks, tennis shoes, warm sweatshirts and jackets to get to the subway. We had to run over rough stone streets to the subway or we would miss it! We arrived and the subway doors flew open, but the car appeared to be jammed with humanity. We tried to squeeze in and were met with glares. I had to make an air pocket with my arms so a little girl who was with us could breathe! She could have easily been crushed by the rude, uncaring subway riders!

We practically fell out of the subway car at our stop, and as we approached the opera house, we noticed some beautifully dressed opera goers arriving in their high heels and mink coats. As they gracefully stepped down from their limousines, one of our jacket-clad friends muttered, "Cruise ship people!"

I slumped in, avoiding eye contact. In the lobby, one of those marvelous Russian contrasts met my eyes: the scarlet velvet couch with gold painted scrolled framework had a spring that had escaped and poked through the velvet cushion! Leaky roofs and now falling apart furniture!

The fitting end to our Russian adventure occurred the next day when our youthful friends took us to a basement bar in one of those gray cement buildings!

We sat around a table with them as they proposed vodka toasts. The men in our group joined them enthusiastically while we ladies raised our glasses. Cautiously, I took a sip. Wooo! That stuff's potent, and strong and cutting as I would imagine nail polish remover to be! I tried to look pleasant and I really appreciated the gesture, but I don't know how they do it! I have heard the government keeps prices low on tobacco and vodka in order to keep the people happy.

We split up at the airport, as some of us added on a trip to Prague, while others went straight home. Prague was such a treat after Russia! It was similar to arrival in Hong Kong had been after experiencing China. We felt free to wander anywhere safely and enjoy food and much more – just like home! When I walked by a restaurant and heard strains of Gershwin coming through the door, I was happy all over!

There was a wonderful carved clock up high on one of the buildings in the open square of Prague. Figures of a boy and girl swung out of it every time it chimed. There was even a muscular guy walking around with a large snake wrapped around his bare chest. We were in a free society, not necessarily my favorite one, but the freedom felt good!

I decided to make one last purchase at the airport

duty-free shop before flying home – a bottle of the perfume Opium. I enjoyed telling everyone at home that I had brought back Opium!

# St. John

My favorite "special island" has been St. John ever since my first trip there. What it lacked is surprisingly what made it everything desirable. In other words, it lacks an airport. It is, therefore, off the beaten tourist track. One must fly into St. Thomas, take a bus to the ferry dock and cross the water in about 20 minutes to the dock at St. John. In other words, you have to really want to go there. Some people of means helicopter in. I was not one of those people!

St. John is my ideal "special island" because it is the most totally relaxing atmosphere I've ever been privileged to enjoy.

Grandparents often treat their families, and you see them all enjoying being together!

Someone once asked about the night-life, and I loved the answer: "Bring a good book!"

I am, however, the lucky owner with Westin of a two week stay in a three-bedroom, two bath suite. I have treated a former friend and my old college roommate and my sister-in-law, plus going several times with my daughter, so I have enjoyed this ownership to the fullest!

Last year, a terribly destructive hurricane carved a huge swathe through St. John's enchanting forest land, land saved by Lawrence Rockefeller, who put it in conservation allowing St. John to avoid the fast and furious development of the other islands and remain pristine.

The hurricane completely wiped out our beautiful Westin, with its condos scattered artistically up the forested hillsides overlooking the beach and beautiful Cruz Bay. Many cottages and billionaires' residences fell to its fury and it's taking years to rebuild. I can't imagine all of my favorite shops, restaurants, high-brow and low-brow hideaways gone – just gone!

I will be the first one back after the "go ahead"!

# Norway

We had a wonderful teacher in fourth grade named Mrs. Sandidge. She kept a well-run classroom and wrote her name so beautifully at the top of the blackboard. I can still see the perfect points on the "W" in "Marie W. Sandidge."

Back in those days, geography hadn't yet been weakened by blending it into an amorphous mass called "Social Studies," which was supposed to mix it in with history. We studied various countries along with their native dress and customs. I remember the Bedouins and Nomads riding on camels wandering endless deserts and the colorful tulips and windmills turning in the Netherlands. At the end of each unit of study, the mothers of my classmates were invited to see art work, crafts, or to hear us sing or watch us dance to a song from that country. Back then, most mothers were at home and thus could come to these shows at 10:30 in the morning! I can still sing "Now we dance like windmills turning; now we bend like tulips gay…" though no one has requested it! I know the rest of the song, but I won't bore the reader.

One fine morning, we studied the Scandinavian countries. What I carried away from that class were the majestic fjords of Norway. They captured my imagination and have carved a niche in my brain for these many years.

I have always loved the water anyway, and the bigger it is the better I like it. Later in my life I discovered that I am descended from sea captains, so perhaps there's a genetic reason. Imagine my surprise and delight when some old friends called and suggested that I join them on a Norwegian cruise! Although buried deep in my subconscious, my desire to see the fjords was still strong!

With their urging and my daughter's encouragement, I made a reservation for a July cruise. This took a bit of nerve on my part as I would be traveling alone until meeting up with my friends, Nora and Jude, in Copenhagen.

The cruise people took care of arrangements, and when boarding SAS in Dulles airport I discovered I was seated in 2A, "business class", which turned out to be what I consider "First Class." I was seated right behind the pilots' quarters! Thus began what was to be two weeks of pampering! I really had no idea of the delights in store for me. It all started with endless champagne and sumptuous dining, followed by reaching down and putting on socks that were furnished and falling asleep in a completely horizontal position – on a plane! I really passed out only to be awakened for breakfast.

All details of the trip were managed beautifully by the cruise line staff. After going through customs in Copenhagen, I went downstairs to retrieve my bag from the carousel. I was met there by a nice gentleman who was holding a sign with my name on it. He helped me get to the Tivoli Hotel, where I enjoyed looking around. They had an interesting lobby with decorations from fairy tales by the famous Danish author Hans Christian Andersen, as well as some life-sized statues of some of his characters.

I couldn't get over the beauty of the young Danish girls behind the counter, so I tried to analyze what was so unique about their looks. I discovered that their blue eyes were different in this respect: the iris appeared to be larger and therefore the pupil seemed smaller. All of that light blue color in the large iris gave them a type of beauty that I kept noticing as I travelled through Scandinavia.

The cruise line had a large staff available to answer questions and help me settle in to my room. They also had delicious refreshments. Nora and Jude, my friends from Milwaukee, called as soon as they arrived. They took a taxi from their hotel to meet me and we had a nice cup of cheer as we began our adventure.

Touring Copenhagen intrigued me. I had never been there and the idea of a bus you could get off and on at any of its stops was appealing. They had several buses making the same tourist loop, so it was no problem and a short wait for the next bus. It was very educational to drive through part of the original city and then the newer part and to see the beautiful harbor. Many people alighted at the park, which featured the statue of "The Little Mermaid" and they later expressed disappointment at its small size. I felt the same way when I saw Broadway ("The Great White Way") and Wall Street years ago! If you hear about something often enough, it becomes HUGE in your mind.

I was favorably impressed with all of the windmills scattered about utilizing solar power. This was my first taste of Scandinavian determination to keep air clean. Something else I found immensely attractive were the repurposed and tastefully remodeled houses in the old section which used to be for the working class but today are modern and sought-after places to live, while retaining the original exterior appearance.

The next day, we assembled to join our group, which was bussed to our magnificent "home away from home," the cruise ship. Our luggage, set out the night before, had magically arrived except for one of Nora's three bags. Being a very seasoned traveler, she had divided their necessities equally between the three bags so that they would never be at a loss for underwear or toothpaste!

Soon we were headed up the gangway to our beautiful, sparkling white ship where we were greeted most heartily and given plastic cards which would serve as identification, suite key and credit card aboard the ship. What a well-thought-out convenience!

When I found my suite, I discovered an engraved invitation next to my door – the first of many – inviting me to a "block party" that night. As the clock chimed five, we were to walk into the hall to meet our neighbors and enjoy delicious hors d'oeuvres, wine and beer that were served by courteous staff members. There was much hilarity and playing "who do you know from my town?" It was a great way to meet new friends!

An introductory formal "Captain's Welcome Reception" was one of the first gala events that set the tone while we enjoyed music played by the ship's orchestra. The tall, handsome captain actually shook everyone's hand and spoke to us – all 750 of us!

The next day we were greeted with 75-degree

weather, so I enjoyed swimming in the infinity pool and catching some rays! There was a very busy pool bar at one end which was the first to open each day. I soon noticed the same older man and his two woman companions decorating the bar stools each morning and ordering "bloodies."

After two days at sea adventure beckoned, and I wanted to go explore Norway.

All passengers received information regarding land excursions in each port we were visiting well before time to travel, so we had signed up and pre-paid for several jaunts that interested us.

The beautiful town of Kristiansand, with colorful marinas, beckoning beaches and the Kanonmuseum was waiting to be enjoyed. The forbidding remains of a large coastal gun battery built during the German occupation of World War Two is now the museum. It was nice to walk around in 75-degree weather, but sad to reflect on the war. The sun shone so brightly on the buildings lining the harbor and felt so good as I wandered. There were many troll statues and souvenir dolls available in the shops. In a moment of lightheartedness, I put on a troll helmet with curved antlers and had my picture taken. Blooming flowers in brilliant hues of red, yellow, blue, purple and orange in hanging pots adorned the store fronts. I piled into a boat with some new friends and sailed around in the sparkling blue water. It was a lovely day!

Next, we were privileged to tour Bergen with its old sailing ships and historic fish market. I had been to fish markets before, or thought I had, but they couldn't compare to these that I saw in Norway. Heaping varieties of many colors and sizes on long tables! Norwegians used to ship them to other European countries. They get sixty percent of their fishing income from January to March.

There was a fantastic cable car ride, the Foybanen Funicular, that took us to the top of Mount Floyen – 1,050 feet above the city – a beautiful city surrounded by seven hills and seven fjords! I held my breath as the car creaked and swayed! I've never been a fan of heights but sometimes I grit my teeth because I love gorgeous views!

We had a unique treat in store when we arrived in Flam. There we boarded a comfortable train, which was proof of the most audacious and skilled engineering feats in Norwegian railroad history! To tunnel through mountains and climb so high took 20 years to build. The train goes through twenty tunnels! The waterfalls and fjords we viewed as we travelled on that train were just breathtaking! We walked uphill to our lunch stop –

an old hotel. It was charming to be sure, but the whole train load of us had to stand in the narrow hallway because there was only one restroom for the ladies and one for the gentlemen!

We learned so many interesting facts from our tour guides at each stop. Who knew, for instance, that only Norway and Japan can legally hunt whales? They say it tastes like beef (hmmmm). They also eat moose and reindeer (look out Rudolph!). The guide added that reindeer are social and loyal to each other, but moose are not. In winter, instead of salting streets as we do in America, they simply pack down the snow and add rocks. Who knew?

I had a strong desire to observe the Norwegian people up close, so I walked into a coffee shop on one of my shore excursions. I was overwhelmed, first of all, by what wasn't there: noise! With four of five tables of people in America, there would be loud conversation. You could have heard a pin drop in that Norwegian place. I took out my cell phone in order to surreptitiously take a picture of the old woman seated at the next table. The lines in her face, under her straight white hair, were deeply etched in her skin, which gave her a certain strength of character. I could imagine how many harsh winters with deep snow and sub-zero temperatures had left their imprint on her forever.

Our stop in Harstad, a town of 20,000, was interesting. They have no sun from November to mid-January, which would keep me from considering residency! They do a lot of ice fishing in winter, but it still wouldn't take the place of a sunny stroll! Since they get 200,000 tourists, I'd say that the season people want to visit must be summer.

On this trip, I found it hard to get used to bright sunlight still streaming into my quarters at midnight, so I was very thankful for the heavy blackout draperies. I loved to draw them closed after taking one last look at the beautiful deep blue water we were gently gliding through! Then I would remove the chocolate mint from my pillow, chew it slowly, brush my teeth and snuggle down on the cloud-soft bed. Ahhhhhhh.

One highlight for me was a wonderful art nouveau museum we came across as we continued farther north. I took many pictures of the furniture, gilded leather wallpapers, graceful stained-glass vases and windows and delicate porcelain. There was so much skilled craftsmanship on display! Before the tour, there was a very interesting film showing the devastating fire of 1904 and the amazing reconstruction of what had been a completely wooden village. The poor villagers huddled in the street, as we saw in the old photos, with just the clothes on their backs! The call went out all over Europe for carpenters, locksmiths, roofers, craftsmen, artists, plumbers, etc. to come to their aid. Europe responded marvelously. The resultant city of today is simply beautiful. Such decorations as roses adorn the exterior of many buildings, and the graceful architectural designs of the eaves is just lovely. Such eye-catching beauty has risen from the ashes!

Soon the big day arrived when I would actually be able to ride on a fjord! Bodo was the spot for this to happen – an interesting place which is the gateway to Norway's true North. We travelled by van to an isolated spot where we went into a barn-like building to be fitted with the proper attire for our adventure: puffy suits, huge boots, goggles and a helmet. I was definitely not a "Calendar Girl!" Then we waddled down wooden steps to sit in our "rugged, inflatable boats." Ours was equipped with a knowledgeable guide. We pushed off and went swirling on these whirlpools created by seawater rushing into a big lake. The guide explained that the seawater finally hits the steep mountainside at the end, makes a u-turn and rushes back out to sea, hence the turbulence. The whirlpools were great fun. Suddenly, we spotted a few sea eagles, which are a rare and protected species. My cell phone was in a zipped pocket and my puffy mittens were another hindrance, but I was determined and finally got one picture!  I captured a distant black speck up high, which was a sea eagle! We also drifted near a lined rock, which dated back to B.C. What a day! It's so hard to get your mind to imagine a time that goes back that far! A truly memorable trip and the answer to my grade school dream!

The next day, we had another interesting excursion, which was to a small church down a winding mountain path. Inside was a faded Madonna painted on wood, which had survived many centuries since Catholicism was replaced by Protestantism in the 1500s. The woman minister gave a good presentation and answered questions. She told us that sermons in towns lasted 60 minutes, but only 30 minutes in the country. The reasoning is that life in town was wilder, so they needed more lecturing! Centuries before clocks, they used an hour-glass visible to the whole congregation, near the minister's head! People would sometimes fall asleep in their pews, so the minister's assistant took a long pole and poked them. Dangling from the end of the pole was a cloth bag with a bell beside it. If one didn't drop money into the bag, the assistant would shake the pole so that the bell would ring loudly in your ear and drive you crazy, so you would drop in  your money to make it stop!

The men sat on one side of the aisle and the women on the other side. The women's side was on the windy side, so they could protect the men. Women who had recently borne a child were separated further by sitting in a special section in the back as they were considered "unclean." Customs are so fascinating!

We were often told on our trip that white paint was the most expensive, and red the cheapest, so we were always looking at the colors of Norwegian homes on our trip. As we slowly cruised past small hamlets nestled against steep mountains, we often counted about 40 or50 homes of different colors. Usually, the main house was white, while dependencies such as the barn and guest house were red and yellow respectively. When parents became old, they often moved to the smaller guest house and married children and their families would move to their big white house.

People who lived in close proximity got along with each other. They had to! Another interesting fact was that everyone flew the Norwegian flag high on a pole when they were in residence! I decided that things must be pretty safe if you advertised that you weren't there when you were away!

I will always treasure my souvenir from that wonderful Norwegian experience which hangs on my office wall – a genuine certificate saying that I crossed the Arctic Circle while on the ship!

# Epilogue

It is clear to me that a great number of events in my life were not random but rather part of a divine plan and that many times out of seemingly bad things came something very good that couldn't have happened any other way! I am so fortunate to have led this life!

Made in the USA
Monee, IL
15 November 2019